As the Sparrow Flies

Experiences of a young eccentric abroad

By Kat Gibson
© 2018

Cover image from an original acrylic painting by K. Gibson

Dedicated to all who have a profound desire to connect in some way with other cultures beyond tourist attraction. May we ever learn, remain humble, and never fall into the trap of believing that we have all the answers.

Contents

Introduction p7

Prologue p10

Part 1 - Guatemala p11

Part 2 - Czech Republic p39

Part 3 - Uganda p52

Part 4 - Rwanda p86

Part 5 - Burundi p108

Part 6 - Turkey p120

Part 7 - Estonia p140

FAQ p149

Post-script p154

Introduction

"Hi, I'm just about to book my flights for Bolivia in a couple of months – just calling to check that all's well and I can go ahead?"

"Sure; everything's sorted our end. There's just one little gap in our notes here – when did you last visit Latin America?"

"I've never been to Latin America before; this will be my first time."

"Ah." Pause. "That's quite a surprise. We assumed, since you made the initial application five years ago at the age of thirteen, that you had been before. We've never seen anyone else prepare with such enthusiasm such a long time in advance of their trip, so we thought you must have lived there before."

"No – I've just been very excited about going, and this is the first opportunity I've had."

Another pause. "Well... Unfortunately we don't send people away to Latin America for a year unless they've experienced the culture before. We want to be as sure as we can that people will cope with it."

"What? I know I'll cope with it. I've spent the last five or six years preparing for it! I've been like a stuck record, talking endlessly to everyone I meet about the upcoming Bolivia-gap-year. I've done countless fundraisers and worked several different part-time jobs to raise the money. I've read so many books about Bolivian culture, and spoken with as many Latin American people as I've been able to find. I've taken Spanish lessons for years in preparation for this. I'm fairly sure I'll cope with the culture."

"Sorry, Kathryn. I know how excited you've been about this, but it's our policy. We can't send you."

Gasp. "Why didn't you say this back in 2007? What do you expect me to do now?"

"Let's see. What I would suggest is that we send you to Guatemala for the Summer, just for a month or so, and see how you feel about it. Then, you can return to England for five or six months to recover from it and process your experiences, before potentially heading to Bolivia next year for six months if you still feel like going. How about that?"

"But I've spent years working towards a full year in Bolivia! Six months there is no time at all – and I'd rather not wait another year before going! And why Guatemala? Could I not go to Bolivia for a month this Summer, and if I 'cope well' with it I could choose to stay there rather than come back to England so soon?"

"No, I'm sorry – Guatemala is what we can offer you. And you'll need the time in between to process it all from a healthy distance, to properly think it through before heading to Bolivia if you still feel up to it. We can't send you there for the full year."

"Is that my only option, then?"

"Well, yes. You can go with a small team to Guatemala. I'll send you some paperwork for it now – there are a few different forms to fill in, and lots of helpful information to read – when we get your forms back I'll book you onto the trip."

I received the paperwork within the hour.

Gosh, what an extortionate amount of money to pay for a one-month trip. Well, if they expect me to wait around in England afterwards to 'process my experiences', they obviously don't know me at all. Let's see what else I can do to pass the time... Ooh, I could see a little more of the world, and visit Europe – and even Africa – and take up friends' invitations to visit! I know it's not really what the organisation had in mind, but this is my year of freedom. I'm finally a grown-up now, so I can use my time how I like!

Prologue

Welcome to the world of my 18-year-old pre-Bolivia travel memoirs.

Each chapter tells of my time in a different country. Each begins with a loosely poetic reflection, followed by stories and musings in more detail. I was not in any one place for very long (less than two months in each country) and can't claim to have any real insight into any of the cultures or places I visited, nor any depth of knowledge about the mindsets of people I met – but found myself deeply challenged, inspired and changed in these short months. Many of my own long-held beliefs, previously-unknown prejudices, ideas and thoughts about life were exposed and wrestled with during this time, and while I may not have 'achieved' anything useful, I learnt a great deal.

The streets, landscapes, buildings and people that became so familiar in those days and weeks are long ingrained in my memory, and still flood back into view when other people mention similar experiences in different places. I hope these short tales convey a little of the feeling, the imagery, even the bewilderment, that I experienced during those bizarre months. Enjoy!

Part 1: Guatemala

Initial Gap-Year Venture

Sacatepequez was my first exposure
To poverty - shantytowns - beside rich grandeur
To bright golden churches; mad drivers galore
And armed military men posted at every door.

We worked in a home full of kids up to eight
Some had been left, just days old, at the gate.
We chopped and cooked veg; we washed sheets and clothes
Took the older kids walking, tickled little ones' toes.

We painted a mural; donated big toys
For fun outdoor play for the girls and the boys
We fed them and bathed them and fed them some more
The laundry produced was an unending chore.

For me, the main challenge was personal space
Sharing 24/7 - we all needed grace!
And conflict and tension which punctured each day
As I tried to respond in a calm, grown-up way…

Then after six weeks working under the sun
We did wonder how much we really had done
Was 'mission accomplished'? Well, what was our goal?
I questioned the impact of our simple role.

The little things still linger on in the mind
Like overfilled taxis; buses one of a kind
And the rain, oh the rain, when it finally arrived
So determined, so heavy, on land so deprived.

I wanted to stay there, to learn and see more
Of the culture and people - so rich and so poor
But was glad to leave when all went to fly home,
To depart from the team and to venture alone.

Chapter One – Guatemala

Getting There

It was the night before my first flight, and I was pumped with adrenaline. I stuffed the last few bits into my old green rucksack, which now tightly contained all that I considered necessary for the full year. My future was calling – I had survived school and would never have to go back; I wasn't even going to wait around for results or graduation ceremonies, and would probably never again live in the town where I had grown up. I was looking forward to an amazing year, and felt rather smug – a well and truly independent woman, finally an adult, ready for a big adventure that I had planned for myself.

At around midnight, my phone rang. It was the retired couple who were to be Team Leaders for the group of youngsters heading to Guatemala.

"Kathryn, where are you?"

"What do you mean? I'm at home, finishing packing. Where are you?"

"We're all at the airport! We're about to board the plane! Why aren't you here?"

Stunned silence. "Oh! I'm sorry! I thought we were flying tomorrow night!" I fumbled around to find my papers. The flight was due to depart at 00:30. Half an hour after midnight. I gasped. What a stupid mistake – I had presumed that it was the evening of the date given, not the morning.

"No, Kathryn! We're about to board now! We'll go on without you; you'll just have to come and meet us when you get here. *If* you get here."

"Ok," I stammered. "I'll try to rearrange my flight and book it for tomorrow night. I thought that was when we were flying..."

"Well, clearly you got it wrong! Didn't you check?"

"Yes, I did – several times. I'm so sorry. I'll let you know when I've re-booked the flight. Hope your flight goes well. See you soon."

Needless to say the Team Leaders were somewhat annoyed with me. I was so thoroughly embarrassed that I considered cancelling the whole Gap Year and getting a normal job in my parents' town instead. Pride comes before a fall. I had been so pleased with myself for sorting out the details myself, but now had to face my parents and admit that I had made this huge mistake.

The mix-up did not come as much of a surprise to my parents, who knew that I can be careless in my lack of interest in details. They had also expressed concern about my terrible sense of direction and very limited knowledge of geography – not a particularly encouraging combination in the life of a naïve teenager about to travel to various countries on her own. One of my secret aims had been to prove to them, and indeed to everyone else, that I could be a responsible adult, independent and free. Clearly I failed at this rather dramatically from day one. My generous and gracious parents ended up forking out the extra £500 to change my flight to the following day, because although I had secured enough money to cover the costs of all the different trips I had not factored in sudden extra costs such as this.

When the flights had been booked for the following night (the time and date that I had originally thought I would fly), I tried to call the Team Leaders to let them know my arrival time, forgetting that they were somewhere over the Atlantic. I left a message, then sent them a text message with the arrival time too, just in case. I breathed a sigh of relief, and a little of my excitement returned, even though I no longer had the security of travelling with the group. I didn't sleep at all that night.

My parents gave me a lift to the local train station at around 9am as planned, and there were various friends there to wave me off. I had hoped to keep my mistake quiet in order to forego any further embarrassment, but my Mum took great pleasure in talking about it to those who had come to see me off, which brought great amusement to everyone present.

At last, I was on the train and on my way to London. There were a million and one thoughts bouncing off the walls of my mind throughout that train journey, and it seemed to last forever. As well as being excited about going to Guatemala and about the year as a whole, I was looking forward to seeing Ben, my then boyfriend, who was going to meet me at King's Cross. He lived a four-hour journey away from my hometown so I didn't see him very often, and I knew I wouldn't see him again for at least several months.

He happened to be in London that weekend, so we were able to travel to Heathrow together where he waited with me until I went through security to board my flight. He had brought all my favourite snacks and more, and he helped me to stay calm despite my embarrassment at confusing the dates, and my nervousness at arriving in Guatemala alone. A week or two later he was to embark on a full year in Bolivia with a different organisation. Although he would be working in a different city, we hoped that we might meet there at some stage once we were both in the country.

At Heathrow I tried to call the Team Leaders again, but again could not get through to their phone. I didn't really worry, presuming that they were asleep and had received the message I'd sent the previous night. I boarded the flight to Atlanta, the first leg of the journey, and fell asleep almost as soon as I had found my seat. I slept right through until we began the descent, then awoke to find breakfast, lunch and a snack on my little table, which I now had to fold away. Very drowsily and feeling a little sick, I ate the food from my lap as we landed.

In Atlanta airport I withdrew some dollars and used a pay-phone to attempt to contact the Team Leaders again. My mobile phone couldn't find a signal – I now discovered that it only worked in England. I wondered whether their phone didn't function abroad either, so perhaps they hadn't received my messages; or maybe they just saw no need to respond and had it turned off whenever I tried to call. Frustratingly I didn't have phone numbers for anyone else on the team, nor for the Coordinator who lived in Guatemala. Lesson learned: always have backup phone numbers just in case!

I found a computer in the airport that people could pay to use, so I looked up the Coordinator's name online and found her blog. I searched for her phone number, hoping to call it from the pay-phone, but couldn't find it. So I tried to email the Team Leaders or the Coordinator, but couldn't log into my emails because I was in an unexpected location. (Gmail tried to confirm that it was me by using a text-message confirmation system – but, of course, my phone did not pick up the messages.)

Somewhat exasperated, I left the computer and went to board the flight to Guatemala. My frustration doubled heading through security when the officials made me remove the ten large bars of Dairy Milk from the very bottom of my tightly-packed rucksack, and it took me quite some time to squeeze everything else back in.

I had wondered whether I would struggle going through security because of my several layers of clothing – but I did not expect to be told to unpack my bag for the sake of chocolate. It was going to be gifts for my various hosts throughout the year. I boarded the second flight rather grumpy, and tired, and with an aching neck from sleeping in an odd position in the previous flight. All excitement was quite forgotten.

As the plane landed in Guatemala I was in a sleepy daze. I felt sick, thirsty and desperate for a shower. Having drifted in and out of sleep throughout that second flight I now felt more tired than when I was in Atlanta. As the wheels of the plane touched down on the runway it occurred to me that there was a strong possibility my original text message had not been received – and that if this were so, I would not be met at the airport. I was right.

Thankfully I did have the address of the Coordinator, which, I was told, was where some members of the team would be staying during our time in the country. So when I arrived in the airport it seemed my only option was to take a taxi to the Coordinator's house. Now was the time to put my A-Level Spanish to the test. I withdrew some money from one of the machines and made my way to the crowded exit.

As I walked, various men approached me from different sides offering taxi services – one of them even tried to take my rucksack from me quite forcefully. Exasperated and feeling almost overwhelmed, I loudly refused them all. I was tired and scared, and was still kicking myself for confusing the dates. I had pain in my neck, back and shoulders, and was conscious that I smelt bad – I had washed as best I could in airport sinks but had not had a shower since leaving my parents' house, which was now two days ago.

Outside the airport it was dark and warm, but there was a refreshing breeze. It was much quieter than inside. When I had calmed myself down a little and practiced some Spanish in my head, I approached a taxi some distance from the building. The driver was leaning on the vehicle with a bored-looking expression and arms folded. I showed him the address on my crumpled piece of paper and asked if he knew where it was. He grunted, nodded and gestured with a wave of his hand that I get in his car.

As we drove I remembered the advice I had been given, to always haggle a price before entering a taxi. Oops. I had been so relieved that the driver seemed to know the address that I had clambered into the car without thinking about it. While we were on our way, the driver's mobile rang and he answered, still driving. After a few minutes of rapid conversation that I didn't understand, the driver handed the phone to me with a shrug and raised eyebrows. I was surprised and a little worried – who was the caller and why would he want to talk to me? Was this normal?

He spoke in simple Spanish, slow and clear, and I stammered my short responses in Spanish too, desperately hoping that he wouldn't say anything too complicated or ask me a difficult question.

"I am the manager."

"Yes. What do you want?"

"I saw you in the airport. White girl, young and alone."

"Yes..."

"Listen. Don't pay the driver more than [an amount of money]. Whatever he asks for, I'm telling you to pay no more than that much."

"Ok. Thank you."

Was this normal? Perhaps I'll never know. I handed the phone back to the driver, who nodded. I imagine he heard what his manager had said.

After driving for about half an hour it became clear that he didn't actually know where we were going, other than the vague region. He began to drive around slowly, stopping regularly and shouting out of the window to ask pedestrians and other drivers for directions. This went on for quite some time. Eventually – after about an hour and a half in the car – we arrived at the Coordinator's house and I paid the amount specified by the man on the phone. I don't remember how much it was; I never bothered to work out what it would have been in pounds because I was so relieved simply to be there, and later couldn't remember the number.

Then I met the Coordinator. Having read snippets of her blog in Atlanta while trying to find her phone number, I was excited to meet this inspiring woman. She had lived in the country for some time and I hoped to ask her many questions about the culture and about her experiences. I looked forward to learning from her. The possibility of not getting on well simply did not occur to me. She opened the door. It was about 10.30pm (Guatemalan time) and she looked quite tired.

"Hi, I'm Kathryn. Have I come to the right place?"

"You! Do you have any idea how irresponsible you've been?"

"Yes, and I'm so sorry. I tried to –"

"You missed the flight, and left the team so worried! It was such an irresponsible thing to do – why did you do that?"

"I made a mistake and mixed up the dates. I don't know how I managed it."

"How could you get the wrong date? You should have checked them! Anyone with any sense would know to check through the details to make sure you've got it right."

"Yes, I'm sorry. I checked but still missed it. A horrible mistake."

"It was so inconsiderate of you. Do you understand that?"

"Yes. I'm so sorry. I was mortified when I realised. I didn't mean to make anyone worry. I'm sorry."

"Of course people would worry! And then after missing your flight you didn't even bother to let anyone know you were still coming! We all presumed that you weren't coming at all!"

"I sent the Team Leaders a text message when I booked,

and tried –"

"Well, nobody received a text message! Did you not *think*?"

"I tried to phone as well, but –"

"Nobody received any phone calls from you either! Why didn't you contact me if the Team Leaders weren't receiving your messages?"

"I'm sorry. I tried to, but I didn't have your phone number and couldn't find it online."

"You were on the Internet?"

"Yes, at Atlanta airport. The pay-phone didn't get through to the Team Leaders either so I used a computer there and tried to find contact details for you. I found your –"

"So why didn't you contact me?"

"I found your blog but couldn't find a phone number there. I tried –"

"Why didn't you email me? My email address is on there for all to see."

"My email wouldn't let me log in because my phone wasn't –"

"And then you show up here, late at night, on my doorstep. What do you expect me to do?"

"Erm, I don't –"

"Well? Did you expect a big, cheerful welcome? After all you've put us through?"

"I'm so sorry. What do I need to –"

"Kathryn, you really need to understand that this kind of mistake just isn't acceptable. You can't afford to have slip-ups like that. It's a cruel world, and people won't just go along with your carelessness and pick up the pieces as if nothing was wrong. You need to learn to take some responsibility."

"Yes. I'm sorry. What shall I –"

"And now you're trying to brush it off and move on. How do you expect us to put up with you?"

"I don't know. I've said I'm sorry – I really am. Should I –"

"Don't you dare answer back to me! You think 'sorry' will cover it, do you? Well, one day you'll have some hard lessons to learn."

She threw her hands in the air and muttered something that I couldn't hear. Then she went into the house, leaving the door open, and started talking angrily on the phone in Spanish.

I didn't dare cross the threshold but felt very awkward standing on the doorstep staring into her house. I didn't know what to do. After several minutes she came back to the door.

"There'll soon be a taxi on the road. Here's the address. You'll have to explain yourself and show them you're sorry; they'll all be asleep by now." She thrust a torn scrap of paper in my hand that had a hastily scrawled address on it, and then went back in the house and shut the door.

I was exhausted. Everything ached, especially my face after fiercely fighting back tears throughout the interaction, and my back after standing there with my rucksack pressing down on me for so long. I desperately wanted to wash. The taxi pulled up a few minutes later and I gave him the address. Thankfully he knew the place, and didn't try to talk to me. Again, I forgot to agree a price. By this point I didn't care. I was relieved to be away from the scary woman, and to have my rucksack finally off my shoulders. I looked at the clock and saw that it was nearly midnight – our conversation had been more than an hour long.

I cried silently in that taxi, genuinely wishing in the moment that I had cancelled the whole trip and got a normal job in England instead. I resented the thought of seeing this woman every day for the month, and dreaded seeing the rest of the team after letting them down by arriving late. I had met most of them a few weeks beforehand at the weekend orientation in England, but still didn't feel like I knew them, and at this point did not have the physical or emotional energy for small-talk and friendly introductions.

It was midnight when I arrived at the house. It turned out that the Coordinator was hosting the two Team Leaders and the two young men in the team; the young women in the team were staying here with a missionary family. The host was still awake doing paperwork and let me in as soon as I knocked. He was as welcoming to me as the Coordinator was unwelcoming, and made me feel very much at home straight away. I breathed a sigh of relief and gulped back fresh tears.

We tiptoed upstairs and he showed me to the room where the four other girls had set out their sleeping bags, expecting them to be asleep. I softly opened the door and found that they were awake and were talking about me, wondering when I would arrive and whether I was alright! I received such a wonderfully happy welcome from them all, and finally felt able to relax.

Starting Work

Although I was nervous about seeing the Coordinator and being chastised by the Team Leaders too, I was excited to start work at the children's home. Thankfully it seemed I hadn't really missed anything – the team had taken the first day to unpack and relax as planned, and we were all introduced to the home together the morning after my arrival.

It was a beautiful place, full of colour and life, with 30-40 children up to eight years old. Their stories varied immensely: some had been sent there by social workers or equivalent; others had been found living on the streets; others had been left at the gate in the dead of night – some of these were just days old. The hope was that each child would be adopted by a Guatemalan family by age 8-9.

The adoption process was not for the faint-hearted, and the government had added further layers of complexity to it for safeguarding reasons in the wake of a series of child trafficking scandals. The rigorous, expensive and generally exhausting process had deterred many willing couples and families, and numerous others gave up part way through. I heard of several recent adoptions that had taken years to complete. A further layer of cost and complication was caused by the fact that the children in the home had not arrived there with birth certificates: each child had to be formally registered and receive a birth certificate before the adoption process could even begin. This was particularly difficult for the children who had no knowledge of who their parents were, or where or when they were born.

Thankfully, our task did not involve the paperwork, though we heard a great deal about it from the staff and the Coordinator. As a team we were split into pairs each day and assigned tasks of cooking, cleaning, preparing food, sorting dirty laundry and putting it into washing machines, sorting and drying clean laundry, playing with groups of children of various ages and leading activities, taking children on excursions, and doing a little DIY and decoration work around the site. Spending whole days chopping carrots or sifting beans was fairly mind-numbing, though I thoroughly enjoyed the days that I was able to spend with the children.

Sorting the clean laundry was the most tiring of all the tasks. The home had recently been given two large washing machines, which the staff showed us with great delight: until a few months before our visit they had been washing everything by hand. Once the washing machines went silent we would unload the wet contents into baskets and walk up four or five flights of stairs, past the children's bedrooms, to the top of a tower block with open walls.

There was a long washing line that formed a narrow oval shape on a pulley system, which stretched from the top of the tower to a pole at the end of the garden below. We would peg up a wet item of clothing on the right hand side of the line, wind the handle to turn the line, and un-peg an item of clothing from the left hand side of the line: by the time the clothes had travelled to the end of the garden and back in the hot sun, they were dry! It was quite a workout, walking up the stairs with baskets of wet laundry and then pegging, winding, un-pegging and folding – by midday the whole body was aching.

Cultural Experiences

Near where we were staying there was a large main road that comprised part of our journey to the home each morning. There was no pavement: we were to walk right in the middle of the road between the two directions of traffic, with four lanes of fast-moving cars on either side of us. This middle lane was not raised in any way and there were no barriers; we felt very exposed. However, we were assured that this was the safest place to walk because we were clearly visible to the drivers. This part of the journey didn't get much easier as the weeks went by.

At weekends we had time off from the home and went on a few tourist trips. We went walking through forests looking at exotic plants and vines; we experienced lovely markets and all sorts of other beautiful places that our hosts took us to. We spent a Saturday climbing an active volcano and toasting marshmallows on the smoke that came out from the hot rocks near the top! We later learnt that the fumes are toxic, and some of us were unwell the following day. One of the young men in the team had brought inadequate footwear and soon regretted it: the rocky ascent was a struggle and the descent was even more so, but on the higher ground where it was hot underfoot his flip-flops began to melt! Even so, we all thoroughly enjoyed the experience.

We also spent a weekend at the famous Lake Atitlan, which is stunning. No photos can do justice to the breathtaking scenery and atmosphere of the place. It's a calm, clear lake surrounded by volcanoes on all sides, and full of colour and life. It was a perfectly relaxing retreat where we could get to know one another better as a team without the pressure of work, and enjoy something of the wonder and beauty of the place.

As well as eating in some fantastic open-air restaurants and tasting wonderful snacks, fruits and drinks, we had chance to hike part way up one of the mountains and have an exhilarating zip-wire experience over the lake, landing on another of the mountains that had equally amazing views. There were eagles soaring just a few feet away from where we were flying, and it was incredible. Bats, lizards, snakes and other creatures made us jump once or twice over the course of that weekend, as did the pickpockets – a wallet was lost which caused some stress, but on the whole everyone found it a truly delightful visit.

At Lake Atitlan we had opportunity to sit and watch the lightning. We had noticed it each night throughout our time in Guatemala, but there was more time to enjoy it while we were away for the weekend. I'm not entirely sure if it was lightning – after sunset each night the sky would light up every few seconds with what looked like lightning, but unaccompanied by any thunder or rain. It was bright enough that we could see our surroundings without street lamps, and it was incredibly atmospheric.

Sometimes back at our accommodation I would sit on the doorstep and watch the sky for a short while, appreciating a few moments of stillness and wonder. Although I'm an extrovert, I did value these precious minutes alone – there was little personal space, sharing a bedroom with four other people. However, each time I sat down to watch the lightning someone from the team would approach me to ask whether I was all right, and then whether I was quite sure. It made me wonder whether other people simply never need any time to themselves.

We only experienced rain once during our stay – it lasted for a few hours and was torrential: none of us dared venture outdoors even for a few seconds. We couldn't see anything through the windows except for the rain itself; it was very impressive.

Another cultural experience was the public transport. The buses were decorated in wonderfully vibrant colours, covered in coloured tassels and painted with cliché phrases in huge lettering. There were no bus stops; the buses would stop whenever someone in the street waved at them or whenever a passenger shouted 'stop'. There was no maximum number of people either – just as many as could physically squeeze themselves into the vehicle, even sometimes hanging out of the door and clinging onto the doorframe. The drivers would often blare out loud music, and some – like the lorry drivers – had larger-than-life photos of the drivers' children on stickers on the sides of the buses.

The taxis, too, were quite different to anything we had experienced in the UK. They would also fit in as many passengers as was physically possible, so when we were travelling together as a team there would often be seven of us riding in a small car in addition to the driver: two on the front passenger seat; four squashed into the three back seats (usually with one on another's knee), and one curled up in the boot. On one occasion our taxi driver realised that he had missed the turning on a fast four-lane road. Instead of waiting for the next turning or roundabout, he simply stopped and reversed until he reached the turning that he'd missed, causing countless other vehicles to swerve around us!

Then there were the Tuc-Tucs, which are like three-wheeler motorbikes with colourful cabins attached to the back. We didn't often ride in those, but on two of our tourist days and weekends away we had chance to try them. On one occasion the driver saw how pleased I was to ride in it and offered me the opportunity to drive for a few miles!

Team Conflict

Unfortunately, one of the women in the team, Sandie (name changed), did not get on at all well with three of the others. They made fun of her, and I saw her crying about it more than once. I was upset by it, too. After talking to the three about it a couple of times to no avail, I was at a loss as to what I could do.

One evening we were all at the Coordinator's house, and as we were clearing up after dinner someone made a snide comment that caused Sandie to excuse herself and leave the room. After one or two awkward minutes I went and found her on the stairs, where she was crying quietly. I sat with her in silence for a short while, and then we both went back downstairs and the evening team-meeting began. Later, when we were back at our accommodation and preparing to go to bed, one of the other girls on the team called me over for a private conversation.

"Just before the team meeting, while you were out of the room, the Team Leaders were talking quite angrily about you. I think they're upset with you."

"That's strange – they seemed perfectly friendly to me in the meeting. Do you have any idea why they're upset?"

"Well, you know during the meal you offered to do the laundry job tomorrow?"

"Yes – I know everyone hates that one, more than the other tasks. I want to keep conflict to a minimum as far as I can, so thought it would make things easier if I offer to do it."

"Earlier in the evening Sandie offered as well – I think for the same reason."

"Oh, that's nice – I don't think I've worked with her yet!"

"But she's the only other Spanish-speaker in the group. If the two of you work together, nobody will have any translation if the staff want to talk to people in the team."

"Ah, of course. I hadn't thought of that – that must be why we haven't worked together so far."

"The Team Leaders looked pretty annoyed. They said your offer was selfish and that you're making unfair demands of the rest of the team. They had a bit of a rant about it."

"Really? But I had no idea Sandie had offered to do the laundry!"

"They thought you knew, and were being deliberately

difficult for some reason. We all told them that you wouldn't think that way; that you wouldn't want to cause problems and would be happy to do any of the jobs. But even though we stood up for you, they still seemed upset."

"Thanks – it's kind of you. I wonder why they didn't say anything to me in person, though. It's a bit frustrating to find out about this when we're back here and can't talk it over with them."

The following morning before work I approached the couple privately and told them that I would be willing to work on any team, and apologised for upsetting them by offering to do a job without properly discussing it first. They looked surprised, and told me that I had done nothing wrong. A mystery!

My worst struggle during our time in Guatemala was with one of the men on the team. Throughout the trip he behaved consistently inappropriately towards me. He kept making sexual comments, and attempting to touch me inappropriately – even in front of other team members. Several times I firmly asked or told him to stop, even on various occasions showing how upset and angry I was about it, but still he continued. Various other members of the team told him to stop his inappropriate behaviour towards me, but each time he just laughed.

I ended up feeling very uncomfortable whenever I was asked to work alongside him without other people present.

Eventually all five women in the team met with the Team Leaders to talk about it and ask advice. The Team Leaders told us that we were imagining it, and that he was a good man. We were to get on with our work and 'stop fussing'. So we tried.

After a few more days of trying to put up with or avoid him as he continued his inappropriate words and actions, the five of us approached the Coordinator about it. She told us that she believed it was my fault, because the man had told her I had been flirting with him. Speechless, I found myself once again desperately fighting back tears. The other women seemed as shocked as I was and began talking all at once about how we had all repeatedly told him to stop speaking and acting that way, that I was not at all romantically interested, and that I had certainly not been flirting. The Coordinator ended the meeting, telling me in a stern voice to be careful.

I was baffled. I even began to question whether the way I talk *had* been coming across as somehow flirtatious. The others assured me that this was not the case. It remained unresolved, and the team member continued to harass me throughout the rest of our time in the country. I kept away from him as best I could, but it was not easy in such an environment – on a number of occasions I was sorely tempted to punch him. I managed to resist, for the sake of team 'harmony'. I really didn't want more conflict with the Team Leaders or the Coordinator.

Towards the end of the trip, the Coordinator was asked by the people in the charity's UK office to interview me, to determine whether I would be a useful asset to the team in

Bolivia six months later. I had not got on at all well with the Coordinator throughout the trip, no matter how hard I had tried, and I wasn't used to this. The knowledge that my desperate hopes of finally getting to Bolivia could depend on the outcome of this interaction upset me immensely.

In the interview, as well as a few relatively normal questions, the Coordinator asked some rather pointed questions regarding my attention to detail, carelessness and disorganisation – though I was sure that I had made no disorganised mistakes since arriving in Guatemala – and questions about interaction with men. I felt like the nature of the conversation was such that whatever answers I gave could be interpreted negatively. By the end of the conversation I felt well and truly put down.

Reflections

On the whole I did enjoy the time in Guatemala. I got on well with most of the team – though was not used to falling out with people and was a little shaken by all the conflict. Perhaps it was brought on by the intensity of people living in close proximity to one another in a foreign culture for a time, or the occasional stress of the work, or the heat, or the language barrier, or a combination of factors – who knows. I enjoyed the work in the orphanage, especially talking with the Guatemalan staff: I was very glad to be able to communicate with them in Spanish. I even enjoyed translating for the rest of the team and gradually growing in confidence with Spanish-speaking.

However, by the time we left I found myself wondering whether our time there had been worthwhile at all – whether we had really done anything, or been useful in any way. We had done some cooking, cleaning, laundry and food preparation, which took some pressure off the staff, but those things would have been done somehow regardless of whether or not we had been there. We were not in the country long enough to form lasting friendships with any of the local people, but long enough to fall out with the Coordinator and Team Leaders!

The idea that we might not actually achieve anything had not occurred to me – as with so many young people going away on short trips to developing countries and hoping to do something useful or play the hero – but it made me wonder whether the experience may have been more about learning and growing as individuals than doing anything in particular.

*****

Some years after the Guatemala trip I bumped into the Coordinator in England and ended up spending some time with her. It wasn't easy, but we get on much better now. At the time of our visit she had been going through a particularly stressful season in her life, and was also not used to having groups of strangers stay in her house. Even though the conversation took place years later, I was thoroughly glad to resolve the conflict – it was like an old weight had been removed from my shoulders that I had kept trying to shrug off but had not quite been able to forget about.

Part 2: Czech Republic

One Monastic Community

Land of peace, of memories so fond,
You taught me to nourish my silence
Surprised me with generous acceptance.
A welcome so gracious; kindness so pure
Hearts dedicated to the Beloved
And unsurprised by His response.
Lives untethered, unhindered, free;
Chastity, poverty and obedience a joy, not a restriction
Rhythms of life leading us ever nearer
To the author of life Himself.
Laughter never far from sparkling eyes
Ever celebrating, ever rejoicing
In the beauty found, the life discovered;
Eager to share the One who bestows it,
Who gives life shape and purpose -
Loving people into His presence.

Chapter Two – Czech Republic

Getting There

The next country on the agenda was the Czech Republic. I had hoped to travel straight there from Guatemala without going back to England in between, but discovered that it was significantly cheaper to fly back to Heathrow with the rest of the team and then to fly on to the Czech Republic early the following morning. So that's what I did.

Not wanting to pay for a hotel room for the 7 hours between flights, I chose a nice spot on the grass outside Terminal Four and lay down to sleep. Before long I awoke, bleary-eyed, to find two policemen standing over me.

"What are you doing here?"

"Err, I was having a rest. I... I've just got back from Guatemala. I'm about to fly out to the Czech Republic."

"What do you mean? Where are you from?"

"I'm from Yorkshire! I've been on a trip to Guatemala with a charity and just got back a couple of hours ago. In a few more hours I'm due to fly out to Prague."

"Why Guatemala? What are you bringing into mainland Europe?"

"Just my clothes and bits – I'm not selling anything. I'm a volunteer – I'm on my 'Gap Year'."

"What organisation are you with, and why are you on your own now?"

"I'm not with an organisation now. I was in Guatemala with a team, sent by a UK charity to volunteer in an orphanage. In the Czech Republic I'm helping out in two churches, with a friend – she's going to meet me in the airport when I get to Prague; she lives there."

"Let's see your tickets."

They watched me suspiciously as I fumbled about in various pockets until I finally found my printed schedule of the year and boarding pass from the flights back from Guatemala. I handed them to the officers, who peered closely at them before giving them back to me.

"Why didn't you go to a hotel between these flights?"

I laughed. "A hotel near here would cost me more than my next flight – probably more than my next two flights! Do I look like I have that sort of money to spare, to waste on a few hours in a bed? That money could pay for birth certificates for several Guatemalan street kids, which would help get them into education and healthcare services! And I don't really do hotels. It's only a few hours – what would be the point in travelling somewhere for a few hours in a bed when I could just as happily rest on the soft grass, here?"

Whoops – my response could have come across as rude, though I hadn't intended to be. I was still very sleepy, and the cost of a hotel in the area seemed an extortionate amount of money to a stingy eighteen-year-old who had been rigidly saving money for years and had very little to spare.

"We don't allow people to sleep on the ground outside the airport."

"But it's warm and dry here, and visible from the entrance!"

"It's against our policy. Go and sit indoors. There are seats there, in the terminal – we can't let you sleep here."

I was tired and frustrated, but went inside and sat for the remaining few hours waiting to board the flight to Prague. It was nowhere near as comfortable as the soft turf, and much noisier.

On the plane on the way to Prague I found myself wondering which college or university to apply to for the following year. By this point I had narrowed down the options to my two favourites, and was confident that I would be offered a place at both if I applied, so as yet I had applied to neither. As I was thinking about it on the flight to Prague, I prayed for some sort of sign. Just as we were coming in to land, I saw through the window a large banner, by the runway, displaying the name of one of the colleges – advertising a film that had the same name! I found myself laughing out loud: this was certainly not what I was expecting. (Incidentally, I did end up going to that college – though not because of this 'sign'!)

Seeking Purpose

Maja (name changed), the friend that had invited me, came to meet me on arrival. The previous two Summers in England we had worked together at a retreat house in the Dales, and had kept in touch. She invited me to come and stay for a few weeks, to get to know her culture and to help out in two churches.

When she met me in the airport, however, she told me that one of them had recently faced a huge conflict and did not want a foreign stranger coming to visit during such a difficult and sensitive time. The other had had a mixup of dates and most of the members were away at a summer conference so did not need a volunteer to help with anything.

As a result, the following day we began looking around the suburbs of Prague and some nearby towns for any organisation that might want a short-term volunteer, one who has no money for accommodation and speaks no Czech. We were turned down a number of times, understandably, and eventually came to a Roman Catholic monastic community who were very welcoming to both of us. They offered free accommodation and food for us on the condition that we live and work alongside the monks, nuns and novices.

Community

The community there treated us as part of the family, which felt like an honour. They even seemed fine with me not being Catholic, and made no obvious attempt to convert me. Communication was difficult – I tried to learn lots of new words and phrases in Czech each day but felt thoroughly embarrassed much of the time because of my inability to communicate effectively. Maja translated for me when she was with me, but we were not always together, and I had many embarrassing moments when I was asked to do something but couldn't understand what it was. Even despite this, I felt wonderfully accepted.

I also gradually began to enjoy the strange inability to chat with people. I am an external-processing extrovert, so it came as a bit of a shock – but over time I began to enjoy my silence and started to notice more of what was going on around me, and to listen more.

For the first half of my stay Maja and I lived and worked there, with one or two day-trips into Prague to see the sights. For the latter half of my visit we had planned to go and see her family. However, one or two days before we were due to go I was invited to attend a one-off meeting in the office of the priest in charge, with various monks and nuns present. I didn't know what it could be about, though wondered whether they were going to ask me for some money to cover the costs of my food and accommodation. Once we were seated, the 'head nun' addressed the two of us in English.

"We wanted to thank you both for the ways in which you have helped out." She looked at Maja. "And we wish you well on your journey to see your parents and your siblings. It has been a delight getting to know you, and we hope to meet you again some time." She turned to look at me. "We have talked and prayed about it, and we would love it if you would stay with us for a little while longer. I know you are in the country for another two weeks – would you be willing to remain in our community for that time instead of going away with Maja? We have appreciated your visit and would understand if you would rather stick with your original plans – but we would love it if you're able to stay longer."

What a shock this was! Although they had not in any way treated me as a burden, I had assumed that the extra challenge of my being there was a bit of a chore for people. Communicating in gestures every day was tiring and embarrassing. But they asked me to stay. They seemed so genuine, so full of love. After a little conversation, I agreed to stay for the remaining fortnight, and the others in the room looked very pleased. I went away and cried after the meeting – I felt so welcomed, accepted and wanted despite the language barrier and all the associated challenges.

After this, Maja left. Throughout our stay I had asked her many questions about why the community did certain things and what the different symbols meant, and she would go and find out the answers for me from the nuns if she didn't know. So when she left, she bought me a small Catholic catechism in English to help me understand more about some of the customs, traditions and beliefs that were alien to me –

and, surprisingly, I really enjoyed reading it.

In the little community, the monks and nuns didn't wear monastic gowns or habits but fairly plain, normal clothes that were shared by everyone. They also wore wooden cross necklaces, two or three inches long, as a symbol of their lifestyle. A huge amount of their time was spent going out and serving in their area – identifying people who were struggling in various ways locally and doing practical things to help out. They put on regular events and retreats for people, too, so the building where they all lived – where I was staying – was often full of people.

Many of the nuns really loved to have fun. I went on various outings with them to social places such as community centres and pubs, where they seemed very much at home and would laugh and chat with everyone. We had film evenings and games nights in the community house too. I'll never forget watching Batman Begins and eating popcorn and chocolates with a group of giggling nuns.

It did not feel at all like what I had imagined of a monastery: it was neither quiet nor serene – except in the Chapel – but fun and full of life. The monks and nuns, although sharing everything, felt very much like 'normal' people except for the immensity of their care and compassion, and their strong desire to serve each other and do some good in society. I was amazed by the sense of love that was tangible there: it was clear that they really cared about each other, and seemed completely unselfish.

Strange Happenings

On one occasion there was a group of about fifteen young men visiting; they came on a Friday morning – the day that the weekly groceries were due to arrive. However, that morning the groceries did not come. The nuns became agitated over what they were going to eat for lunch and what they were going to feed the guests – there was nowhere near enough food left in the house to feed the monks and nuns, let alone the group of visitors as well. The monastery van was away on an errand and there was no other vehicle available to drive to the shops to buy more food; nor were any shops or supermarkets within walking distance.

After phoning various people to no avail, the nuns concluded that all they could do was cook what little food they had and feed the visitors a small snack-meal, and the monks and nuns could fast until the evening – by which point the groceries might have come. So we prepared the food, knowing that it would not be enough to sustain the group, but there seemed to be little else that we could do.

It was a strange meal: bits of leftover veg, a couple of cans of soup, a few leftover sausages, all cooked together in a casserole with some herbs. Once it was ready, we put it on two trays and slid them into the enclosed pulley system that went between the upstairs kitchen and the dining room below, and one of the nuns prayed over it. Another was downstairs ready to distribute it to the tables where the young men were seated.

What happened next has baffled me ever since. Somehow, the visitors all ate and were full. Once they had left the room we went in to clear up after them, and found that not only were there leftovers on every table, but there was enough food left over for the twenty-odd monks and nuns to have large portions and eat more for dinner that evening! It was very strange – there seemed to be a great deal more food left over than what we had prepared to begin with, but it was the same food as what we had prepared.

Nobody was quite sure what to make of it. At first there was quiet confusion, with puzzled expressions on everyone's faces, and then the nuns began asking each other questions and looking between the tables and the hatch – and then after a while began talking in quiet excitement, whispering and giggling with huge smiles and raised eyebrows in obvious amazement. All the nuns seemed quite bewildered but very happy, and kept thanking God.

Celebrations

During my last weekend there, there was a huge party to celebrate one of the nuns making a lifetime commitment to the community. There were speeches, hugs, prayers, many colourful decorations and a vast amount of delicious food – it was wonderful. And after all that I had experienced over the course of my time there I found myself loosely considering the possibility of joining the community too! I figured, however, that Ben probably wouldn't appreciate it, and of course I had other things to think about.

*****

A year after the trip I heard from Maja that she had joined the community and was now living there, having been deeply impacted by the two weeks that she had been there with me! She remained there for a couple of years, and then ended up marrying one of the young men who was staying as a novice with the monks during my time in the community. How life changes! After the trip I kept in touch with the 'head nun', too, who spoke good English. She later moved to Poland and served a monastic community in the same order as this one, and I went to visit her there for a week about a year later, after returning from Bolivia. Wonderful people.

Part 3: Uganda

Most Memorable Week

Bewildered stumbling over that dust ocean
In Equatorial heat sliced roughly by jagged shade.
The air, like my mind, thick with confused requests;
Strange questions unraveling the fabric
Of cultural understanding.

Offering weighty cases of irrelevant secondhand gold;
Lodging in a place that added fuel to the fire
Which ever cried, 'She's laced with wealth and it's yours for the asking!'
Bombardment by begging men in suits
With smartphones and cars.

Fabricated statements the embroidered blanket of misplaced trust;
Cold reality an unrefreshing splash in the face.
Miscommunication or misunderstanding or plain falsity?
Here stands one naïve Mzungu, afraid and unaware,
Who must comply.

Small in stature yet painfully aware
Of shocking skin, interpreted as a boast:
Inherent knowledge, superior ability, unwanted power,
Woven with perceived riches
Beyond imagination.

A ghost am I, a hairy-armed phantom
With imposed duty to teach and preach and instruct.
Such obligation a backpack of bricks.
Can blue eyes knit words for the dying,
Desolate, desperate?

But even bricks an exotic luxury
I'd ever taken for granted, alongside good health.
My needlessly decorated culture in such stark contrast -
Speechless I carried the unavoidable assignment
To preach.

Homes crafted of few found sticks, insufficient scraps;
Iron sharpens iron, yet unmade windows gape.
An Eeyore's house so often rebuilt,
Empty of all but perhaps a blanket, and a few
Suffering bodies.

Children adorned with one threadbare garment;
Holes limply joined in mud-stained rags:
What was once an ill-fitting t-shirt
Now covers little, exposing skin
Hung from bones.

Then at nightfall determined crowds
Wandered from villages that seemed stranger still
For the pleasure of the ghost-girl's shouted nonsense;
From a distant land yet owned by the same
Creative Deity.

Tens, now hundreds - dancing then standing shoulder to shoulder;
Wide white eyes of children peeking out from the trees -
Oh how I longed for their company instead
As the shouting began and my despairing heart resumed
Its seat in my throat.

Then the nightly return to a bed in a house:
Toilets, electrics, water, solid walls.
Bitter tears at the taste of my own hypocrisy;
And a woman had washed and ironed
My clothes.

Chapter Three – Uganda

Transport and Accommodation

During my week in Uganda I was staying in a village near Kampala, but spent the late-afternoons and evenings out in more rural villages about an hour's journey away. Most of the time I travelled by "boda-boda" – motorbike taxi – I'll never forget my first ride in particular. I was lifting my leg to get on the bike behind the driver, when he stopped me with a shocked expression on his face.

"No, miss! You sit sideways."

"Oh! I don't know if I'll be able to balance if I sit sideways. I've never ridden on a motorbike before."

"You can balance. You cannot sit facing forwards; it is not decent."

"Ok." I climbed up onto the bike and sat sideways behind the driver, feeling pretty wobbly. "Like this?" He nodded and turned the engine on.

Frantic, I felt under the seat but there was nothing to hold onto; everything under there was burning hot. I couldn't even get a grip on the edge of the seat with my fingers. I was getting increasingly nervous. "Excuse me – what can I hold onto, for balance?"

The driver laughed. "You can balance. Don't touch under the seat – your fingers will burn."

"Where should I put my feet?" There was nothing for me to rest them on, and I could feel the heat of the bike against my legs, so I knew I couldn't rest my legs against the bike.

He laughed again. "Do not burn your legs on the bike, or your feet. Your shoes will melt. You can balance – all the women do that. Are you ready now, Miss?"

I shook my head, desperate to find something to grip with my hands or feet to stop feeling so precarious. The driver grinned. "You will be ok. I will drive carefully for you."

As soon as we set off I found myself clinging onto the driver for dear life, which he laughed at and people we passed frowned at. I really don't know how people do it – legs dangling in the air with nothing to rest against; nothing to hold onto and no way to stop oneself falling off the bike – it was terrifying!

If balancing wasn't difficult enough with these restrictions, the driving added to the challenge: speeding along with great confidence on steep and bumpy dirt roads as if it were a game. We lifted off the ground several times, and even skidded fair distances down steep gravel or dust slopes. It didn't get much easier over time; I dreaded these daily rides, every time convinced that I would fall off and injure myself. The adrenaline was immense. On several of my journeys I was spoken to about holding on to the driver, but I felt that there was little else I could do to keep from flying off the bike.

During my stay I would have liked to have access to a working phone or the Internet, to talk to family and close friends about what I was experiencing – but in hindsight I'm glad I didn't, as it would have caused unhelpful worry. I had known in advance that I wouldn't be able to get in touch during this time, so had told people not to be concerned if they don't hear from me. Ben had said that he would be praying for my safety during this time, and I found myself very glad of it.

I was, however, able to process my experiences to a certain extent in conversation with my hosts, and ask their advice. They were a friendly English couple in their early sixties. They lived in an 'international boarding school' that they had started some years earlier with the aim of breaking down some of the rich-poor divide in the city. They were offering free boarding and education for street children that they found who wanted to learn, and paid boarding and education for families who could afford it and who wanted their children to be taught in English, from an English curriculum.

From what I could gather, it seemed to be hugely successful in its aims, and they noticed little segregation or envy between the children. I was sharing a bunk room with various children of primary-school age, and woke up to them singing loudly every morning in the room. It was an inspiring, if somewhat tiring, place to stay, and I loved being there. They even had an indoor toilet and cold running water, which felt like such luxury. The couple were good to talk to and eager to help me learn about the culture.

The Organisation

Alas, the boarding school was not the reason for the visit, though at times during my stay I sincerely wished it had been. For a few years I had received invitations from another small organisation that run educational events in fairly remote villages teaching hygiene and various life skills, and work in orphanages. I had come into contact with them through Facebook and had been inspired by their work – and they kept on asking me to come and see firsthand what they do. Eventually, since I was now planning to be in East Africa anyway at this particular time, I said that I would come over for a week to visit and watch them at work.

It transpired that the people who had invited me, who had organsied my schedule (and who had expected me to ride Boda-Bodas with as much confidence and balance as any local person) had never before worked with any foreigners. They told me that for this reason they had been hugely excited to meet me. During my visit I was taken out to fairly remote communities in which many of the residents said they had never seen anyone from outside Uganda, let alone a white person – and some were convinced I was a ghost.

In light of this, perhaps it is no surprise that we miscommunicated regarding a number of things before I arrived in the country.

"We have booked a room for you in a Western hotel in Kampala, for when you visit us. Here is the bill for your stay there."

"Thank you for looking into this – however I can't afford that price. Is it possible for me to stay in someone's house? I'm more than happy to sleep on the floor somewhere."

"No. You are white. I will find another Western hotel for you with a better price."

"I don't think I need a Western hotel. If there is nobody that could host me, maybe I could stay in a cheap hostel of some kind; something that local people use?"

"No. You would not be safe; you would catch diseases. We must keep you safe. Here is a better price for another hotel where white people stay."

"Thank you for your concern, but I still cannot afford that price. Is there anything significantly cheaper that would be available?"

"Not something that would be safe for you. You need to stay in a Western hotel. You have money for it – you are white!"

After quite a long time talking about this and beginning to stress a little, I found contact details for the couple that ran the boarding school. They were friends of people I had met in the UK, so I asked if I could stay with them and was glad to hear they had a bed available. The Ugandan men that I had been communicating with seemed shocked that I would not stay in a hotel, and bewildered that I was willing to stay in a bunk-room full of Ugandan children. They continually refused to believe that I couldn't afford a fancy hotel.

The same men also told me that they had a concern for church leaders in Ugandan villages. "These pastors and ministers have no access to the Bible. They need the Bible desperately. You must help us."

"Wow, it's surprising that they don't have access to it. What can I do to help?"

"We need money for Bibles. They are 35,000 Ugandan Shillings each, or $10. This includes transport 'costs so that someone can buy them from the city."

"I didn't realise you wanted money from me. I don't really have any money to give towards this, I'm sorry. I've told you already that I can only just afford my flights and things, and don't have money to spare. Maybe the churches in Kampala will help with this is you ask them, or if the pastors and ministers ask them?"

"They will not help us. Can you bring us some Bibles from your country."

"I wouldn't know where to find Bibles in Ugandan languages here, and I imagine they'd cost more here as well."

"People in our country understand English. Your country is full of old Bibles that your people do not read. Bring them to us, for our pastors and ministers. They will read them."

By this point I had already left the UK. So, while I was in Guatemala, on a borrowed laptop one evening I sent out messages to various churches, Christian friends and organisations in England, asking people to donate any unwanted Bibles so that I could bring them to give to these church leaders in Ugandan villages.

I managed to organise it so that people could post their old Bibles to a friend of mine, who would put them into two large, unwanted suitcases and bring them to Heathrow for me to collect on my changeover day between the Czech Republic and Uganda trips. I booked two one-way checked bags from Heathrow to Kampala, and so far everything went fairly smoothly. My friend came to meet me in the airport and gave me the heavy suitcases, and I managed to get them to Kampala.

However, when I arrived and handed them over, I learnt that nobody in the villages we were visiting spoke English. I also found that church leaders who did speak English already had Bibles, and that most of those who complained about not being able to afford them had smartphones, cars and large televisions of their own. I felt like such a fool, and didn't know what to trust – or indeed what to say to those who had helped with this in the UK.

Another odd miscommunication related to timekeeping.

Each evening I was told, "Someone will come and pick you up on a boda-boda at 10am tomorrow." And each day, someone came to meet me – not at 10am but at 4pm. Three times I asked them to clarify whether they really meant 10am, or whether it was likely to be later – but again I was told 10am, and again someone would show up at 4pm.

After the first few days of this happening, I began using my time more productively. I started helping in Maths and Geography classes in the boarding school from about 9am until 3.30pm. It was great fun, and I learnt a lot from those children! I appreciated having something useful to do as well, and stopped feeling guilty about lodging there for free.

When I did go out to the villages, except for the time travelling on boda-bodas and with a few exceptions, I felt very well looked after by those who worked for the organisation. They were constantly looking out for my wellbeing, especially making sure that when we were staying in one place I would sit in the shade as much as possible rather than standing in the sun. "We have heard stories that you might turn from white to red. We cannot have you turning red like the rumours say – you must stay in the cool shade."

However, from their perspective the purpose of my visit was not, as I had believed, for me to see their work in person and watch them do the things that I had read about on their Facebook page. Having discovered that the organisation had never before had any dealings with westerners except through Facebook, I soon realised that they thought the colour of my skin made me capable and qualified to do almost anything. For example, I was expected to preach at open-air crusades.

For at least an hour every evening, I was pushed onto a makeshift stage and told to preach, with a translator. They would not allow me to use any notes, and most nights I had to shout as they had no amplification – though on three evenings they brought a microphone and a generator (one needed a microphone to be heard over the sound of the generator!). Hundreds of people would gather to listen. I had no choice in the matter, and despised it!

"I can't preach. Please don't ask me to do that. I'm no good at public speaking, let alone preaching – I really don't know that I have anything useful to say to people. And I haven't had chance to prepare anything!"

"You don't need to prepare. Be led by the Sprit. We never prepare for the messages we bring. They will be glad to hear whatever you say to them."

"But I honestly wouldn't be any good at preaching, and I don't feel able to do it. I really don't want to do this. Please don't force me to preach."

"You have come here, all the way from England – you must have something to bring to us. People are excited about it."

"I am not excited. I had no idea that this was what you wanted; I thought I'd be visiting orphanages and educational events and the like, not outreach crusades! I'm not a preacher."

"Here is the poster. All the villages in the region have seen it. They are looking forward to hearing you speak and bring a message for them." He showed me a poster, with a picture of me on it – taken from Facebook – and some words that I didn't understand. I couldn't bring myself to ask for a translation.

"Why didn't you ask before putting me on a poster? I really don't know what I can trust at this point."

"We cannot let people down. If you do not do it, we will all be put to shame. This shame will change everything. People will stop supporting us. Our orphanages, all our community events and our educational programmes will have to stop. Our families will suffer, and many families in our region will suffer. The children will have to go back to the streets if that happens."

Needless to say, I had to do it; I was given no option. I had a painful throat and little voice left by the end of the week. And, of course, I was asked for money by people from the organisation several times a day, "because your country is very rich", and, "because you saved money from not staying in a hotel". When I said I didn't have anything to give, they said, "ask your family and friends – they will be kind to us".

Poverty

I noticed that in the capital city and the areas around the outskirts of the city, many of the children would approach me and beg, while in the villages further away I saw nobody begging in this way. Instead, crowds of children would simply follow me wherever I walked. In some of the areas near the city the houses had patchwork tin roofs and often just one very old-looking mattress shared by a family of seven or eight who would live together in one room with very few possessions – and yet, several of these houses would have a TV! I found it quite a shock to see that the TV would take priority over other possessions like beds, food, crockery and potentially-life-saving mosquito nets.

In the farther away communities where we spent the afternoons and evenings, there were certainly no TVs. The poverty there was beyond anything I had imagined, and I was very shaken by it. Many of the houses were made largely of long sticks or bits of branches with the twigs cut off, and patched up with pieces of cardboard, metal or fabric – often with big gaps. I was told that many of the people in these villages had no possessions except for the clothes they were wearing and perhaps a blanket. Cooking pots and buckets for washing were shared between several families, and children were dressed in adult-sized t-shirts with nothing else underneath, sometimes with gaping holes in the seams.

The smell in some of the villages was almost overwhelming, too. I was told in particular areas that people there did not live long, and after hearing in some detail about a few of the health conditions people were suffering with, I didn't have trouble believing it. I was bewildered, lost for words and incredibly upset by what I saw. Why was the nearest health centre so unreachable or unhelpful to people here? What would it take – what could be done, and why weren't any charities helping? I wondered about the possibility of buying things like blankets, pots, buckets, secondhand clothes, mattresses, soap and the like to bring for people, but cringed at the stereotype of the naïve white girl coming in with this sort of aid – and I certainly didn't have the money to buy things for everyone; there were so many people.

It's impossible to express quite how much I resented the obligation to preach in these villages. What on earth was I supposed to say to people? How could I possibly think I had anything of value to offer, when I knew nothing of their lives, struggles, families, culture; when I was so alien to it all? And why did the men from the organisation think that bringing in a stranger from a faraway land to preach would be useful to them in any way? Who knows. Perhaps in my narrow-minded naïveté I was too blinkered by the poverty and disease that I saw; perhaps the people in the villages were much more able than I was to look beyond these perceived barriers – perhaps what they really wanted was encouraging words, 'spiritual nourishment', inspiration and the like, just like anyone else.

I tried to find courage in this: of course, the people in those communities are people just like anyone else. Even if they were coming to the events for an evening of bizarre entertainment – a nervous, young foreigner looking somewhat uncomfortable, standing on some wobbly pieces of wood and shouting strange things with the help of an enthusiastic translator – I would play my part. It was not my place to let them down after what they had been promised, regardless of how I had been let down by those organising the events.

Still, I hated having to stand up and say something. But I had no choice. I would be pushed onto a roughly made stage somewhere each evening, and then return at night to a brick building with running water and electricity. I felt like such a hypocrite.

It turned out that in addition to these evenings, I had also been advertised as the keynote speaker at a three-day pastors' training conference at the end of my stay. I know very little about the work of pastors, especially in Uganda, and at the age of 18 with no training or experience I felt completely ill equipped to teach them. Although I said so numerous times, the men from the organisation simply kept on telling me not to be modest and to trust in God. *Argh!*

The one positive thing about the pastors' conference was cabbage! Until this point, my every meal so far – including at my accommodation – had been 'posho and beans': African black beans in a thin sauce, with a flavourless white paste made from maize flour and water. At the pastors' conference we each had a small amount of cabbage in the bean sauce, which was wonderful! I have never before or since been so excited to eat cabbage, and the pastors looked very pleased too: they all got up and danced when the food arrived.

Meg

Meg – who had a much longer Ugandan name but asked

me to call her Meg – had come to some of the evening events with the men from the organisation. I think one of them had asked her to come as some female company for me. I appreciated it! She spoke English fairly fluently and had answered some of my questions about the culture, which I'd found very helpful. She had asked me many things about my culture, too.

One afternoon, she had brought me to see her house. She lived in one of the slums on the outskirts of Kampala, in a little house that she said she had built with the help of a neighbour. She had an old wooden table, and there was a dirty-looking sponge mattress rolled up on the floor underneath that appeared to have worn thin and had holes in it.

She introduced me to some girls who were in the house.

"Do they all live with you?"

"Yes – I have eight girls now."

"Gosh, you don't look old enough!"

She laughed. "I have never had a husband, or had any children of my own. But I am old – I am nearly twenty-eight, so I think I will never have a husband. But these are my girls. I really hate to see children offering their bodies on the streets just to pay for food. Often if they cannot afford to eat, girls will become prostitutes as it is easy to make money that way. But I will not allow it in my area. When I see a child doing this, I ask her if she would like to live with me instead. So now," she laughed again, "I have eight!"

"Wow, what an amazing thing to do! Do they all sleep in here, with you?"

"Yes. We put the table on its side at night. The five younger ones are happy with a blanket on the floor; three older ones sleep on the mattress with me – but sometimes I am on the floor as well. We don't mind; we are very blessed."

"Gosh. How old are your girls?"

"The youngest is seven; the eldest is sixteen. We have become a nice family now; we all look after each other. I teach them right and wrong – I teach them that it is not good to have sex with lots of men. I teach them good moral values. They like to learn. I've taught them to sing and dance, too, and to forget life's troubles."

I looked around, and couldn't see any cooking equipment. "Do you eat with other people?"

"There is a stove outside that all the houses in the area share. I work as a dance teacher now, and I can afford for me and my girls to eat a good meal together each day – we have posho and beans."

"Ah, you're a teacher – does that mean the girls can go to school?"

"We cannot afford to buy uniform or books yet, so the

school will not take them. But every month I ask the school to give me some old books, worksheets, pens and things so that the girls can learn. They do not usually give me anything, but sometimes I find good sheets and things in their bins. It is my dream to send my girls to school one day – I know they are clever, and they deserve to have a good future."

I really wished I had money to buy them a new mattress and some school supplies. I was later able to put her in touch with a friend in the UK who began sending money each month so that the girls could go to school and buy some of the things they needed – but at this stage I didn't know that this would be possible, and felt powerless to help her.

Saturday

On the Saturday night, the final evening of my stay, the organisation had planned the largest of all the open-air events of the week. They had been looking forward to it immensely. I had not. Incidentally, on that same evening, one of my favourite American musicians was doing a world tour and happened to be in Kampala, less than an hour from where I was staying, and my hosts were going to the concert! Due to unexpected illness they had a ticket available and a spare seat in their car, and they offered it to me for free. I had dreamt about seeing this musician live, but had never before had the chance. And he was here in Uganda, at the same time as I was!

I'm torn. I certainly deserve some time off. I've earned the right to go and have a good time, just for one evening, especially after what a struggle the rest of my week here has been. But I know it would be a huge letdown to the people in this strange organisation, who for some bizarre reason are counting on me to be the keynote speaker for their big event. Maybe I've got the right to let them down and go to the concert – after all the times they've misled me, manipulated me, placed overwhelming demands on me, pestered me for money... But they've been so excited about the Saturday evening event. I'm not sure I have the heart to bail on them – and I don't really want to see their reaction if I were to do so either.

Slightly upset and quite resentful, I decided to go to their event as planned. I felt like maybe, possibly, I might have done the right thing – but who knows.

People arrived and started to sing and dance from 10am, I was told – though I didn't get there until after midday. I was travelling by car with Meg and one of the pastors. Every twenty minutes or so of the two-to-three-hour journey a police officer at the side of the road would flag us down in order to have a conversation with the 'Mzungu' (white person), and we were obliged to stop and chat until each officer let us continue. When we finally arrived I sat in the shade and watched the wildly expressive improvised singing and dancing, feeling far too tired, hot and self-conscious to consider joining in. I was being stared at.

Throughout the afternoon and early evening people would tentatively approach me and prod me – apparently to check that I wasn't a ghost – or stroke my skin, or pull my hair. At first I found this funny but it quickly began to irritate me.

Eventually the sun started to set, and I became increasingly nervous. I dreaded having to get up on that stage and come up with things to say for an hour, especially in the knowledge that this particular evening would have even more people in the crowd waiting expectantly for me to spout something meaningful.

I looked around to try to guess who my translator might be for the evening. There had been several different ones so far, and I often wondered how accurately my words were being translated. Often people would cheer or dance at seemingly odd moments, and I was never quite sure what had been said to provoke this.

Throughout the week, I had noticed the various pastors and leaders saying things that I profoundly disagreed with. I decided to use that Saturday evening to address a few of those. In part, this was probably because I was resenting not being at the concert – *if they want me to preach then they'll have to put up with what I want to say*. I was fed up of dancing to their tune.

One example is this: I had heard people saying over and over again that when people become Christians, life ceases to have problems; that God fixes everything immediately. They said that if a Christian has a disease and is not suddenly and miraculously healed when they pray, it must be a sign of the person's lack of faith or the insincerity of their conversion. They also said that God wants to bless people with abundant finances, and that becoming a Christian would make their businesses successful.

Whenever I heard these things I felt so angry and upset about the damage that these mindsets could cause, and had arguments with two of the pastors about it. That Saturday I spoke my mind, in front of several hundred eager listeners, and read out various Bible passages to back up what I was saying: that sickness and poverty are not a result of people's sin or lack of faith – that God does not promise health and wealth to all, but to be with people in their struggles.

I assume I annoyed most of the pastors and Christian leaders. Two of them told me afterwards that they didn't like what I said, and one claimed to be speaking on behalf of all the other pastors too. I took comfort in the fact that Jesus regularly upset the religious leaders by things he said to the crowds.

Several other people approached me in tears that evening, thanking me again and again – they told me they had believed that their poverty and sickness was their own fault for not having enough faith, and they had been carrying immense guilt as a result on top of it all. I was glad that I could speak out for them, even if it did aggravate their leaders a bit.

Another thing that had frustrated me about these evenings was what they called the 'ministry time'. During the evening after some music and dancing there would be a five or six talks of ten to twenty minutes by various people, and somewhere in the middle I'd be pushed onto the stage to speak for an hour (whenever I tried to get off the stage after speaking for only 30-40 minutes they would push me back and tell me to speak some more) – then came the 'ministry time'. This involved all the pastors and Christian leaders getting up onto the stage and shouting aggressively over the people standing below.

I was shocked! On the first evening I asked my translator what was going on, and he told me that they were cursing the Devil. *Who are these people? What could they possibly be trying to achieve?*

The following day I approached one of the pastors.

"Could you tell me about your 'ministry time'? Why do you all shout so angrily from the stage, all at once? I've never seen anything like it before."

"We are expelling the demons from the people. When the demons are gone, then they can be healed and receive a blessing from God."

"Is this something you do regularly?"

"Yes, every time we hold an event we do this. It is important – if we don't cast out the demons, the people cannot receive from God."

"Ah. So if you hold events in the same place twice, does it mean the demons have come back in between the two events, so you need to cast them out again – or do you just do it once?"

"No, we do it again and again. The spirits are strong in

these areas, and God has commissioned us to fight them. This is why we show how strong, loud and angry we are – the Devil needs to know that we are prepared to fight, and that God is stronger than all the spirits."

"Can the spirits not hear you unless you shout, then?"

"We need to be loud, to show them our strength."

"What about the people – do they not get scared by all this?"

"No. People know how important it is that they are liberated from the Devil. After the demons have gone from them, then they can receive blessing. Don't you do this in your country?"

"Maybe some people do, but I haven't seen it – at least not like this. We would prioritise talking to God rather than talking to demons. Wouldn't praying for the people do the same job? Can't God get rid of the demons himself if you ask him to?"

"God has given us a loaded gun – spiritually speaking – and he wants us to use it. If you were in the front lines of a battle and you saw the enemy troops approaching, you wouldn't go to your commander and ask him to get rid of them for you. You'd use the weapons you have!"

I found it pretty scary to watch, and it seemed to me that nobody really enjoyed this time except for those on stage doing the shouting. The whole practice made me uncomfortable, but for most of the week I told myself not to make a fuss about it since I have so little understanding of the culture.

On the Saturday night I decided to try something a little different. I asked the pastors and leaders whether they would like me to lead the 'ministry time' that night, in a new way. They were surprised at my offer but cheerfully agreed.

When the time came and the pastors began pouring onto the stage, my translator sent them down and reminded them that I would be doing something different. They looked at me with confused expressions, apparently presuming that my plan had been to stand at the front of the stage and join in with their shouting. However, they reluctantly sat down at the edge of the stage as I spoke briefly about how anyone and everyone can talk to God, and that he listens regardless of whether we shout or speak normally, or even whisper. People seemed surprised, and after a few moments there was some whooping and cheering.

Then I encouraged them to pray for themselves and for each other in groups of 2-3 people – to tell God what their needs are and what they're thankful for; to say whatever they wanted to say to God. People seemed to enjoy doing this for about ten or fifteen minutes, and became rather animated praying for one another. It was very loud, and the crowd was rather squashed.

My translator acted as a sort of heat-shield between myself and the pastors, several of whom shouted at him during this time. I was thankful to him for not translating very much of what was said, other than, "They don't like it." However, surprisingly, they did not take over by force or stop the people from praying together.

After this, I called the children to come near the stage. This seemed to shock the pastors even more. At the start of the gatherings each evening the children were sent away to play in the trees; they were not to disturb the adults under any circumstances but were to keep themselves to themselves. This had irritated me hugely, but once again I had told myself not to make a fuss about it since I had so little cultural understanding. Again, I decided to try something different on the Saturday evening.

When they came out from the trees and gathered by the stage, I told them the same thing that I'd told the adults: that they can talk to God if they want to, and that God cares about what is on their minds, regardless of how loudly or quietly they might express it. They seemed very excited by this, and one of them asked, "Does that mean we can pray for people?" I nodded, and asked if they'd like to try it. This seemed to really animate them – so after the noise died down, I invited people from the crowd to come forwards if they want someone to pray with them, and encouraged the children to go and do so.

These ideas – that we don't need to shout; that we can talk to God and do not need to just keep telling demons to go away; that even children can pray – seemed to come as a shock to people in the crowd. However, many of them had intrigued and expectant expressions on their faces. The children chatted to one another with huge smiles and a huge amount of energy. People began to push their way to the front of the crowd where the children gathered around in little clusters to pray for them.

This somewhat different form of 'ministry time' seemed to go well, from what I could tell! Afterwards there was some singing and dancing for half an hour or so, and then one of the men who had been organising the events told me to get in his car. I asked why, but there was an unfamiliar urgency in his voice, so I did as he said. He drove me back to my accommodation, and told me that he would explain the situation the following morning.

The next day, he picked me up from my accommodation at 9am (on time, for the first time during my visit!), and I asked why I had had to leave the village so suddenly the previous night.

"You saw how large the crowds were at the event. People had walked from several miles around to be there – many people from the surrounding areas had been excited that a Mzungu was coming to preach to them. But the witchdoctors did not like this."

"Witchdoctors? I didn't realise those still existed – I thought they were just in stories from many years ago."

He laughed. "No, many villages still honour them, but not in the same ways as they used to – and there are certainly not as many as before. In some places they still have a lot of power and people listen to what they say. Sometimes they do not like our events; when people become Christians they do not always continue to honour the witchdoctors or listen to them, so they do not like us."

"Did they come to the event last night, then?"

"Yes. Several of them from the region had gathered together and made bad plans, so we had to make sure you were safe."

"What kind of plans?"

"To take the Mzungu preacher away. To show everyone that their power is the greatest; that they are still in control. They believe that consuming Mzungu skin would enhance their supernatural powers."

I gasped. "Surely that's not true. They wouldn't seriously have abducted me in the middle of a big event, would they?"

"They felt that they needed to prove their power and strength, and give people a warning not to follow the Christian way. I have seen them do similar things before."

"But how did you find out about this plan?"

"We recognised them, near the end as people were dancing. We saw them standing around the edges of the crowd. I am ashamed that we did not notice them sooner – I don't know how long they had been there, but when we saw them they were starting to close in from different sides, looking at you. You had to go back to the city immediately; that is why I spoke so urgently and did not answer your questions."

I was very shaken hearing about this, and was glad that I hadn't been told the previous night. I didn't know quite what to believe.

Sunday

I was due to leave the country in the late afternoon, and since it was a Sunday I was told that I would be visiting a church. I felt relieved that I wouldn't have to preach any more, and could just visit and relax. When we arrived the service was already in full flow. After two or three songs which were accompanied by some wonderful dancing, the man at the front of the church proclaimed an enthusiastic greeting to "our sister from the west!" – then looked at me expectantly, and sat down.

My driver, who had told me in the car about the strange events of the previous night, led me to the stage and stood beside me to translate. I gawped at him.

"You didn't tell me this would happen," I hissed. "I thought we were only visiting!"

"You must preach now. Thirty or forty minutes – that's not so bad."

I was completely unprepared. After stressing for a few moments, I decided to read the Lord's Prayer. I read through it line by line, and talked about the different things that each line or section could mean or represent. This was well received, and I was relieved at the end when we finally left the building and got back in the car. To my bewilderment, I then discovered that we were not driving back to my accommodation but to another church, about a twenty-minute journey from the previous one.

This church seemed to me a strange and wonderful structure. Some long, relatively straight branches of trees had been cut and tied together with ropes to form the shape. There were no walls or ceiling, just these fairly spindly, rough-cut branches marking out the corners and indicating where the walls and ceiling should be. We had to walk along planks of wood about 15cm wide through a boggy area of long grass before reaching the structure; it was quite an adventure! There I was told to preach again – "Something different for this church."

From there we went to another church, where some children performed a few dances for people to watch, and afterwards I was expected to preach yet again. In total we visited five churches that day, one after another, and it took us a couple of hours to drive back to my accommodation afterwards. I don't think I'll ever know whether any of the churches had anticipated our visit, or whether they simply saw a Mzungu visitor and therefore expected me to speak: that was the impression I got. It was an intense day, though I probably would have enjoyed it if it wasn't for the preaching.

In the evening Meg took me to the airport on the back of a boda-boda, and took the opportunity to give me a brief drive-around-tour of Kampala on the way. It felt like quite a culture shock after spending so much of my time out in the rural villages. Although my accommodation was on the outskirts, I had not really seen or explored the city.

She showed me the large buildings, expensive hotels and restaurants, conference centres and monuments. One of the buildings she pointed out was a large, modern church. I saw the name of the church written in large letters on the building, and knew I recognised it from somewhere.

"This church is famous all over the world, for their choir. They go on tours in many countries – they have even been to your country several times."

"Ah, yes! The choir came to my town a year or two ago. I didn't go to the concert, but someone I knew was there and said the group told many emotional stories. I heard they raised a lot of money in donations that evening because of the stories they told about poverty and disease. People liked the music, too."

"Yes, they are very good musically, since each of the members has had specialised vocal training. But the other churches don't like this church. They spend so much money on music training, flights and a fancy sound system, instead of serving the poor. They ask for money for the poor, but then spend it on their building, and on a big extension to the pastor's house. I hate the thought of people all over the world giving their money to help those in need, when it goes into the pockets of the rich."

I found this a bit of a shock, having never before come across this kind of 'miscommunication' regarding charity finance – it made me think a great deal.

*****

All in all it was an amazing week. I met some incredible people, made some big mistakes, learnt some important life lessons, saw some really beautiful scenery and breathtaking sunsets, and saw more eagles than I could count. I was amazed to leave the country alive and healthy after all the scary motorbike trips and the like. If I had known in advance what it would be like, there is no way I would have gone – and I would not repeat that week for anything. But I would love to go back. Uganda is an amazing country, and I'd like to spend more time there, learning from the people and the culture.

Part 4: Rwanda

Survivors' Village

A wide, grey river wanders
Lazily as the clouds
With innocent face concealing
Those silent stories.

Exclusive diet of banana beer
Masks the outcries within
Numbing the desperate despair
Dissolving past and future.

Many curious eyes and voices
Pursue at a small distance
Bare untiring feet still unsought
Many miles from home.

Their soft shouts and energy
Soothed, cooled, the day's intensity
As cold water to the face
Lighthearted; made it bearable.

Tangible, defensive emptiness
Stiff hopelessness hanging in the air
Clinging persistent as disease
Whispering, "Give Up".

We visited a memory
Fabric scraps piled in a corner
Once worn by many with pride or shame
Now simply to draw breath.

Yet hope was chosen: a future
We spoke out of inexperience
Of survival, childhood and goats
Then spontaneous dance for rain.

Chapter 4 - Rwanda

After an incredibly intense week in Uganda, travelling to Rwanda was a relief, and felt almost like a rest. In Rwanda I had a bedroom to myself; electricity most of the time – even Internet access for about half an hour a day! Such luxury.

I was staying with friends, an English couple in their late twenties who had lived in Kigali for several years. They were the only foreigners in the charity they worked for, among around twenty other staff members. I had the pleasure of spending time with different colleagues and being introduced to many different areas of work both in the capital city and further afield.

When I arrived in Kigali, after dropping my bags off in their flat my hosts treated me to Mr Chips, the fast-food place around the corner from where they lived. I cannot begin to express what it was like to eat a burger and chips after a week of just 'posho and beans'. Throughout my time in Rwanda the food was fantastic (no more burger and chips after that first day!). Boiled meat, potatoes, rice, black beans, baked and roasted plantain, various other things – it was wonderful.

In the City

Kigali is a wonderful city, bustling and full of life. At the time of my visit the government had recently introduced new health and safety regulations, which looked rather bizarre to an outsider. One example was that the men who drove the bodas (motorbike taxis) were to wear hair nets and helmets, along with the passengers – but in practice many of the helmets were broken or were swinging from the front of the bike rather than worn, and the drivers wore shorts and flip-flops.

Things like helmets seemed rather out of place on roads where you regularly see whole families piled onto a single bicycle: the father pedalling, a child sat between the handlebars, the mother sat behind holding two children in her lap. Of course, I was used to seeing this kind of thing on motorbikes, but on bicycles it was a surprise! Similarly there were many cyclists balancing huge baskets of goods on their heads as they rode, or washing machines – I even saw one man cycling with a full-sized fridge-freezer on his head.

My first few days in and around Kigali were spent visiting the various children's projects to get a feel for the work. There were a number of schools and a few children's homes to see, and I learnt about their sponsorship programme: people in the UK can send money each month to cover a child's school fees, food, clothes, toys and books.

Once a month the sponsored children meet together in a large centre for a day of activities. They sing songs, play games, receive any letters or gifts from their sponsors and write letters in response with the help of translators. I went along to one of these and spent the day serving food, chatting with some of the children who spoke English, helping them write letters, distributing gifts to the right people, and listening to their singing.

A significant part of my time in the city was spent doing administration work in the office. It took me a while to get used to the coffee that they drank there. On one of my first days I was offered a cup of coffee, and about ten minutes later was presented with a steaming cup of something very spicy that I'm convinced did not actually contain coffee. The flavours were so overwhelming that I felt like my nose and my brain were exploding at the same time. After a few tentative sips I decided that I couldn't possibly finish the cup, but was desperate not to offend those who had made it – so I did something that I've never done before or since, and poured some of it into a nearby plant-pot when I was alone.

Afterwards I was mortified, and desperately hoped that I hadn't damaged the plant – thankfully it seemed fine and did not show any signs of problems. After that point when people offered me a coffee I would either politely decline, or ask for it with some extra hot water or milk to tone down the flavours until my taste buds got used to them. This helped tremendously, and by the end of my time in Rwanda not only could I happily drink a whole mug of the stuff without feeling like I was exploding, but began to actually enjoy it. Success!

One of my tasks in the office was to open packages from sponsors, check that there were no 'inappropriate' gifts within, and sort the gifts into boxes to be sent to the different regions where the kids lived. I enjoyed this, especially seeing the some of the bizarre things sent among the heartfelt gifts from sponsors.

I had to remove things like GameBoy games (none of the children in the projects had games consoles – most of their houses have no electricity), packets of condoms (sent for children!), English tea bags (many of the local people found the concept strange: tea is usually brewed in pans with leaves, herbs and spices), penknives (I've no idea how these got through international post), paracetamol, toy guns, packets of cigarettes and more. I had to laugh – I'm sure the sponsors had good intentions, but I did wonder what they could possibly be thinking in some cases!

There were some beautiful letters though, with family photos, life stories, anecdotes about colleagues and pleasant everyday things. People also sent lovely gifts such as handmade clothes, knitted toys, little musical instruments, sweets, children's books, hair clips, stickers, coloured pencils, notebooks and the like. It made me wish that I could afford to sponsor a child, especially after having met many of them and seen what a difference it makes to their lives.

School Work

While I was visiting one of the schools, I was asked to help with a few classes. It was an International School, with classes taught in English: the children there learn English as a second language and by the time they finish primary education can speak and write it fluently. Helping there was great fun – the children were so energetic and eager to contribute; quite different to what we see in English schools! I was also involved with marking essays, which was almost as much fun as helping in the classes – I found many of them very entertaining and learnt a lot about the culture from them.

One of the assignments, however, left me perplexed and concerned. It was entitled 'How to find a spouse'. The girls' essays were all very similar, and went along these lines:

"There are two different ways of finding a husband: the way of the world, and the way of God. The way of the world involves dating different young men until you find the right one. The way of God is better: a young man finds an attractive girl who is caring and good at housework, and after watching her for a little while he arranges for their fathers to discuss marriage. If they agree and an exchange of gifts is agreed upon, the young man proposes to the girl – and she says no. If she were to say yes straight away she would be considered 'easy'. The second and third proposals, over the course of a few weeks or months, she also rejects – although if she is desperate to marry the man she might accept the third proposal. The fourth she accepts, otherwise she would be considered rude and ungrateful, and would bring disgrace on her family."

I was shocked, and wondered how much choice the girls have in the matter – and whether there was any possibility of girls befriending boys with a view to potentially dropping hints about proposals, though there was no mention of this in their essays. Several of the boys' essays in answer to the same question continued the story and shocked me even more.

They wrote that after finding an attractive, thoughtful and hard-working girl, and after having the fathers agree on the gifts, and after proposing to her until she finally agrees, the young man will get to know her quite well and get stuck into wedding preparations – then will ask her whether she is HIV-positive. He would know at this point that she is likely to give an honest answer. If she says no, he will happily marry her and have many children by her. If she says that she is HIV-positive, however, he will leave her immediately and find another young woman to start the whole process again with.

Both the boys' and the girls' essays were written in a very matter-of-fact way, without questioning the process at all. I was stunned. The betrothal gifts had already been exchanged! The wedding preparations were in place! You cannot just *leave*! I found myself crying, for a long time, for all those young women whose fiancés had left them in the middle of the wedding preparations, not only breaking her own heart but also bringing shame on her family and leaving everybody from both families in debt from cancelled arrangements.

I tried to put myself in the shoes of the young men, to understand how they could possibly behave with such cruelty. Of course, if he were to marry the hypothetical HIV-positive woman, he would have to live with the awareness that she could suddenly get seriously ill and die, at any moment: she could live for decades, or only weeks. He may contract it, too. What's more, it is a deeply rooted part of many African cultures that a man's honour is tied up in how many healthy children he has – but the couple's children, too, may be HIV-positive.

That, then, is the decision: a sword-of-Damocles lifestyle that may end up full of pain, disease, bereavement and death, or simply leave the fiancé and look for a safer option. The latter may leave both families in debt, be considered a disgrace, break her heart and bring shame on her family – but he would avoid the terror of HIV. What a choice.

Gifts of Hope

I was also involved in distributing 'gifts of hope'. There are various websites from which people in the UK can send money to buy particular things – cows, goats, chickens, farming equipment, school books, bags of maize flour, pans, mattresses and the like – and organisations in other countries purchase the chosen items and give them to people in need. The charity I was with ran one such website.

We were to buy the specified items from the market and deliver them to families that we were told had great need. Almost every recipient cried when we brought the gifts. Nobody was expecting them, nor had asked for them; it was a complete surprise.

At times I felt myself cringing as we reinforced the stereotype of 'rich white people giving aid to poor Africans' – but I was glad that the gifts would make a positive difference in people's lives, at least for a while, so I tried to shake off the feeling. I remembered some of the communities I had visited in Uganda and how much I had longed to be able to give something helpful to the people there who had so little in the way of possessions, and was glad that this sort of programme was thriving.

When I asked about community development work, I was told that the gifts often have a long-lasting impact and that people use them to benefit those around them, so that whole communities are strengthened. The charity often hear people who have received the gifts talking enthusiastically about being able to help others and serve their village in a new way.

Change of Plans

Dear Kathryn,

We have some regrettable news for you. Unfortunately, there has been some conflict among the staff at the home in Bolivia where we had hoped to send you, which has led to the volunteer coordinator leaving the region. As such, they are unable to take on any more foreign volunteers until they have found a new coordinator and reached some stability, which may take years. We apologise sincerely for the frustration and inconvenience that this must cause you.

We would like to offer you a voluntary position in a project in Brazil instead. Attached is some information about it – I hope you'll find it inspiring. Let me know if you would like an application form to work for this project.

Yours, Luke

Receiving this, while I was in Rwanda, was somewhat stressful. I had been preparing to go to Bolivia for the past six years and couldn't bear the thought of not making it there in the end. Incidentally, a few weeks earlier I had emailed the organisation that Ben was soon to start working for in a different part of Bolivia, to make contact out of courtesy. On the same day that I received the stressful email, I also happened to receive their reply.

Dear Kathryn,

Thank you for your message – it's great to hear from you. We are very much looking forward to welcoming Ben as a volunteer in our boys' home soon, and to getting to know him as he settles in. Please do come and visit when you reach Bolivia if you find yourself with some free time; we would love to show you around the projects. And, of course, if your plans happen to change at all you would be more than welcome to come and volunteer in our girls' home.

We wish you all the best and look forward to hopefully meeting you at some stage. Roger

This was quite a surprise. I read through the information on their website and began to get excited as their work seemed to be more suited to what I had wanted to do than the project that I was originally going to work for. I replied to let them know the dates that I was available, and asked for details regarding what the work and the accommodation would involve. A few emails later I agreed to work for them.

A further benefit to working for them was that it worked out immensely cheaper than the larger charity that I had originally planned to go with – it saved me several thousand pounds! I was baffled and very happy. Within a few days I had signed up to sponsor a child in Rwanda, thankful that I could now afford it.

I arranged to meet with my sponsored child, and to bring her some gifts from the market: flour, soap, a notebook, coloured pens and a few other bits. Spending a day getting to know her was absolutely wonderful, and it was exciting to know that through this sponsorship she was able to start attending school and have regular medical checks and the like. I still write to her and love to receive her letters and drawings.

Genocide, and Parenting

Throughout my time in the country I heard a great deal about the 1994 genocide; it was mentioned regularly. I was told that until a couple of decades ago certain harmful beliefs and suspicions were so deeply ingrained in everybody's upbringing that it was impossible to undo the mindsets that had caused so much destruction.

Hutus had been raised with the belief that their Tutsi friends and neighbours may turn against them at any time and grasp opportunities to kill – the attitude that 'if I don't kill him, he will kill me first'. Tutsis had been raised to believe the same of their Hutu friends and neighbours. How can a whole nation live with such suspense, waiting for an attack from their companions, believing that they may have to strike out against people they love in order to defend themselves and their families?

Even while I was there, long after the official end of the genocide, I was told that these attitudes still remain in some people. I imagine that the vast majority were relieved that it had 'finished' and would grasp the opportunity to live in peace and security, learning to trust one another – though apparently this was not universally shared. People told me that their country felt like a sort-of-safe place, but that there was tension hidden just under the surface that sometimes showed its face. Of course, things are infinitely better than they were, and for this we can all be thankful.

I had opportunity to visit a memorial on the way to one of the villages. It was in an old church building, a plain stone structure that had been converted into a sort of disorderly and unmanned museum.

It was full of hundreds of skulls in display cabinets, and large piles of bloodstained clothing lying in the corners of the room. I was shocked to learn that during the war many Hutu officials had spoken with the vicars and pastors and priests, instructing them to invite Tutsis to find shelter in their churches, and that they (the officials) would then come to the churches and kill everyone there.

If the church leaders did not comply, they would be tortured and killed, along with their families. So, appallingly, many did comply – and churches became 'safe places' for Tutsis to find refuge, until the Hutu officials came there and killed them all. They did not come with guns; they came with clubs and machetes. I was told that babies were held by the ankles and swung around, and their heads smashed against walls; and that pregnant women were sliced open on the church altar. Children were raped in front of their families, and then cut into pieces with machetes. Family members were ordered to kill each other or be killed more brutally themselves.

I was speechless and felt very sick just being there and hearing all this, surrounded by the bloodstained clothing and shelves full of the skulls that had been found in that very church. Since those days, although being a Christian is acceptable, wearing a cross has been seen as an insensitive, even offensive reminder of the atrocities committed by so many church leaders during that period.

There were reminders everywhere. We would drive down any road and a Rwandan colleague would point at a building and comment that it was where his brother or uncle or cousin had lived before he was killed with a machete, or that the relative's own children had killed him on the doorstep under orders from officials. Friends turned against each other; next-door neighbours looked out for opportunities to attack and kill one another. It was shocking, barely believable – and utterly impossible to forget. It is good to remember, if it means that we are less likely to repeat these horrendous events – but for those grieving there is no relief, anywhere.

Those who were known to have committed the worst genocide crimes were later arrested. Because the prisons were far too full, the government developed a system by which those people could give the names and locations of all they had killed, and if any living relatives of the victims were to come forward and publicly forgive the killers, they might receive a shorter sentence.

I met a woman whose whole family except for one brother had all been murdered by one man, a neighbour of hers. She had gone forwards and publicly, legally forgiven the killer. She said that since everyone had seemed to be killing everyone else, she reasoned that perhaps it wasn't personal.

This shocked me hugely. How can slicing people up with machetes be 'not personal' – especially your own neighbours, whom you grew up with and whose children played with your children? Still, she forgave him and he was soon released. As soon as he was released, a few years before my visit, he hunted down the one brother whom he had left alive, and killed him. He returned to prison as a result.

The woman spoke about it with a blank expression on her face, as if she had been trying not to think about it or remember the details; as if it was now simply information. She had since got married and had a child – she had 'moved on' and started a new life; she tries to keep the grief of bereavement in the past, just like everyone else. Almost everyone now in the country over 30 was bereaved because of the genocide and has horrific memories of that time.

On the way to one village we crossed a bridge over a murky river. I was told that during the war many bodies of Tutsi people – as well as some live but injured people – were thrown into it. People said that the river should carry them to the Nile: 'back where they came from'.

My hosts told me that up until the genocide one's tribal identity could completely change depending on various factors. I was told that if a man had many cows, he could easily become known as Hutu, even if he was Tutsi by birth. I heard that if someone was tall and lanky he was usually Tutsi, and if someone was shorter and had a wider nose, he was probably Hutu. They said that when the genocide was at its worst, some people would kill by guessing a person's tribe by looking at their appearance. Imagine being targeted for the shape of your nose, or for being tall.

There were a few villages that had been described as "survivors' villages", two of which I visited to help with parenting courses. These are places where, a few years before the genocide officially began, prominent Tutsis were sent to live. They were villages where the land was barren and nothing would grow, and survival was difficult. Disease of many kinds spread quickly in these places, and I was told that the stench of death filled them even before the genocide.

Because the villages were completely populated with Tutsi people by the early 1990s, during the genocide Hutu officials who were known to be HIV-positive were ordered to go to those villages and rape those living there. While not everybody was killed, all were attacked, and people who survived the genocide and continued to live there developed all kinds of health conditions, as did their children after them.

In one of these villages, because there were now barely any jobs in the area and little for people to do, I was told that the men spent all their time producing and drinking banana beer. The smell of it filled the air throughout the whole village. All the men we encountered were drunk, at 11am. As ever, children followed us wherever we walked – though these children seemed quite different to children from the other areas. There seemed to be a tangible sense of hopelessness and despair.

On the way to help with the parenting courses I asked what would be taught during the day's session.

"Oh, the basics."

"What are the basics of parenting? I've never been one – I know nothing about it!"

"Well, in this village we have seen that mothers are leaving their babies and young toddlers to fend for themselves. They do not wash or feed them. We will encourage them to do so."

"Surely they know that in order to live their children need to be fed! Everyone knows that!"

"Maybe they do not want their children to live. Maybe survival is not worthwhile in such a cruel world. We hope to encourage them to try, to keep trying, and to hope for a better world in which their children may thrive."

"Wow. So, how will you do this; how will you encourage them to hope for their children's future?"

"We will tell them stories of other communities that have transformed through hope, dedication and hard work. We will help them to celebrate what they do have."

"And what do they have, that they can use to develop the community?"

"They say they have nothing, but it is not quite true. The parents tell us, 'We have no food to give our children' – because no plants will grow and they have no animals for meat. But they do have a little maize that somebody brings for them. And they have goats! We noticed that wild goats wander the outskirts of the village. We have suggested that they eat goats' meat and drink their milk."

"Why don't they do that already, if they have goats?"

"They tell us that goats are unclean animals, and that many people would rather die than touch or eat goat, or drink the milk. We will encourage them to think differently and to try it. It might just keep them alive, and will help with their health."

The course seemed to go well. We sat in the dusty ground in a space between several little houses, that had a tree for some shade. I later heard that after we left some people in that village began to feed the children goats' milk and to eat the meat. The health benefits became obvious almost immediately and others followed, until this particular village became known locally for their 'disgusting habit' of eating goats' meat and drinking their milk. But, seeing that some of the children were living longer and looking healthier, I was told within a year that one or two other villages followed.

During one of the parenting courses, at one point we began to feel a breeze (again, we were sat on the ground outdoors), and the women became quite animated. As the wind picked up and the dust started to blow around, people began making excited noises, and some got up to dance. The teaching stopped, and everybody seemed to be chattering loudly and making celebratory noises.

"What is this all about? Why are they dancing and cheering like that?"

"They are hoping that the rain might come."

"Why is that so exciting?"

"Here, it has not rained for more than three months. They hope that today is the day. If it does rain, some will take it as a sign of hope – and some will remember the parenting course very vividly because of it."

It did rain, very heavily indeed! Some people stayed outdoors and danced in the storm; others sat under a nearby roof and sang, and shared stories. By this point everyone seemed happy and chatty – what a change it was from the hopeless and depressed atmosphere when we first arrived.

When we left at the end of the day, people shook our hands tightly and thanked us over and over again for caring, and for the advice we had given about health and hygiene. I'll never know how much of that was just cultural politeness, and whether they were really going to put into practice some of the things that had been suggested. Perhaps time will tell – though I will probably never know.

Part 5: Burundi

Speechless

Burundi – oh, those mountain views
So vast and bright with greens and blues
To walk up there in English shoes
I'm speechless.

Guards at the door protecting me
A house so open, light and free
Without electricity
I'm speechless.

When driving up that long main road
At corners lorries rarely slowed
I'm told that there, blood often flowed
I'm speechless.

The cyclists held on to the rear
Of cars and bikers, without fear!
I couldn't help but shed a tear
I'm speechless.

Burundi – oh, those mountain views
So vast and bright with greens and blues
So painful now to hear the news
I'm speechless.

Chapter 5 - Burundi

The visit to Burundi was the shortest of all my trips: just four days. I took an overnight coach from Kigali in Rwanda to Bujumbura in Burundi, and then a boda-taxi to the village where I was staying – then the same in reverse at the end of the four days. I wanted to see and experience the culture, and learn more about charities that I had been in touch with there, but unfortunately didn't leave enough time to see or do very much.

Arrival

My host met me at a community centre near his village and took me back to his house on the back of a motorbike, where his wife welcomed me with a wonderful cup of tea. She chatted with me for a few minutes as he sorted out a few things outside, then she left to see to the kids and he came indoors. He sat down, clasped his hands in his lap and looked fixedly at me.

"Now, I need to make you aware of a few things regarding your appearance. First, trousers. Don't wear those around here."

"Ah, I'm sorry – I didn't think about it! I've been wearing trousers to travel, though have some skirts with me. In the villages I visited in Uganda and Rwanda women are expected to wear skirts."

"Yes; here too. You really should have changed into a

skirt before leaving Bujumbura. People in my village will have assumed that you're a prostitute. No other women in this region wear trousers."

"A prostitute? Are you serious?"

"Yes. It's –"

"Wow, I'm so sorry; people will have seen me on the back of your motorbike! I hope this hasn't damaged your reputation in the area!"

He laughed. "Indeed. People are fairly used to me doing strange things – we're the only Mzungu family in the village and we haven't quite embraced all the cultural norms yet – but it's still a bit of a concern. Also, those earrings give a similar impression."

I removed them immediately. "Ok. What do earrings mean, then? And does it count for all earrings?"

"Well, small studs are fine – but anything that hangs below the earlobe is also a sign of prostitution in our area."

"Flip. Ok, that's good to know. What else do I need to be aware of?"

He grinned. "You might want to take your bracelet off, too."

"For the same reason as the earrings? Does the

prostitution thing apply to all jewellery?"

"No – that's just dangly earrings. Bracelets are considered to be a sign of witchcraft."

"Surely you're pulling my leg." I laughed – but he was deadly serious.

"Nope. People in our region are very spiritual, and very superstitious. Many people here practice witchcraft, and they often mark it – so as to identify one another – with bracelets of different colours. You stand out enough around here as a Mzungu; it's really not worth drawing extra attention to yourself by dressing like a prostitute who practices witchcraft."

Accommodation

I spent three nights in Burundi: two in the house of this English family, and one in the house of some American charity-workers I met there. Although the two buildings were more Westernized than other houses in the area, and the one where the Americans were staying was brick-built, there was no electricity in either. They told me that there was occasional electricity in the family's house but that at this time of year it was rarely accessible. This meant that we went to sleep when the sun set at about 8pm, and got up with the sunrise at around 5am.

We had candles to guide us through the house when it began to get dark, which was my first experience of having to live by candlelight. It felt both exciting and peaceful, and I thoroughly enjoyed it.

The family's house was very open – there were low walls about two feet tall and then semi-transparent bamboo walls from there up to the roof. It was wonderful: we could feel every little breeze, but were not too badly scorched by the sun. We could watch the outside world go by, without being entirely visible to the outside world unless people looked closely – which many passers-by did.

The family also had a guard, a friendly man who sat just inside their front door drinking tea and listening to the radio. He was very cheerful, had the most delightful laugh that rang out loud and clear at regular intervals, and was great fun to talk to. My host told me that it was necessary because there were seemingly random attacks on the area, which were getting increasingly frequent.

He said that there were strong repercussions from the Rwandan genocide on top of general civil unrest in the region, and that as a white family they were an obvious target. Several of their neighbours had strongly advised the family to hire a guard for the safety of their children. They enjoyed being able to provide someone with the employment opportunity, too – and the guard had quickly become very close to their family. He would often explain elements of the culture to them or teach them what they needed to know in order to get on well with others in the area.

In the other building, where I stayed my final night with

the three American charity workers, we spent the evening chatting by candlelight and went to sleep an hour or two after sunset. Above my bedroom there was a small attic space of some kind, which felt strange to me since I'd become used to being immediately below the roof at all times: very few other buildings in the area had any stairs, ladders or extra space below the roof. I was told that the land-to-population ratio was such that there was no real need for people to build tall houses except in the big cities, and bungalows are structurally easier to build.

However, my American friends were staying in a house with a small attic which could be accessed via a ladder, and during the night I could hear what sounded like dogs running around up there. The sound of running, slipping and scrabbling on the rough wooden floor, often followed by a loud thud and silence for a few moments before the running resumed, kept me awake almost all night. In the morning I asked them about it.

"How do you sleep, with that racket above your head all night? I've just about got used to the sounds of the insects throughout the night – I found them horribly loud at first but at least now I can more or less sleep through them – but that running and scrabbling was intense! Are there dogs up there?"

"Ah, we thought that when we first moved in, too. We discovered to our horror that they're not dogs; they're big rats."

"Rats? How can rats make that sort of noise? The beasts up there are heavy!"

"Yes – they're huge. We barely slept a wink for weeks when we first found out; pretty terrifying creatures. We've tried to remove them so many times, but it hasn't worked – nobody's been able to do it. Our neighbours tried to help, but the rats have won so far. There are no local pest control companies that can help us either; we really need to find a professional from another region if we can afford it. It doesn't make living here particularly easy, especially at night. But hey, at least we're not concerned about them chewing through any cables – there aren't any!"

Visiting Projects

My hosts took me to see various projects run by a few different charities that worked together, in and around the two major cities. We travelled between Bujumbura (the political and legal capital) and Gitega (the traditional trade capital), and the road between the two was terrifying. It is known as one of the most dangerous roads in the world. The scenery was breathtaking – the most beautiful views I had ever seen – but I found it hard to breathe as we drove beside a sheer drop for much of the journey, lined with countless ribbons tied to sticks in cross-shapes as memorials to those whose vehicles had fallen there.

There were cyclists who, on the long up-hill parts of this road, would grab onto the backs of lorries and cars in order to be pulled along. Other cyclists would ride up and hold onto the backs of the seats – or t-shirts – of those cyclists and be pulled along too. Thus it would escalate: we would see lines of seven or eight cyclists holding onto each other and the one at the front holding onto a car or lorry. If one were to wobble on a pot-hole or lose his grip, those behind him would fall.

Many of them were transporting goods, too, carrying large bags or heavy objects on their backs or heads. If these were to fall and hit the rider behind, who knows how many cyclists and drivers might be affected. Different people quoted different percentages regarding the number of deaths out of all the people who travelled on that road, and the average number of deaths per day there, but I tried hard not to think about those. It really was a terrifying experience – numbed slightly by the contrast of the fantastic views.

My host was heavily involved in various ways with children's projects and innovative social enterprises, but would also go off on long trips on his motorbike every so often. He loved to visit very rural villages to meet with local leaders, witchdoctors and other fascinating characters, and would come back with all sorts of incredible stories. He was full of entertaining anecdotes relating to cultural mistakes that he had made and strange things that had happened.

Return Journey

The trip back to Rwanda at the end of my time in Burundi was very memorable. I had wondered whether to pay the extra money (the equivalent of about £6) to take the 'VIP coach' from Bujumbura to Kigali rather than the cheaper option, but I was stingy and didn't think there would be much of a difference between them. How I regretted my decision later! That long overnight coach journey was rather frightening.

The driver appeared to be heavily intoxicated, and almost constantly swerved around the road, even when we were driving beside very steep drops. We were traveling at high speed, and every minor bump or pothole seemed to almost lift the vehicle off the ground. I spent most of the journey desperately praying for safety, convinced that something would happen to the coach. Other passengers seemed calm (and I was the only foreigner as far as I'm aware), though some were shouting and seemingly arguing. Some slept. I did not.

When I got to Kigali, shattered and quite smelly by this point from fearful sweating throughout the night on the coach, I took a boda-taxi from the Kigali coach station back to where I had been staying with the English couple. Part way through this leg of the journey a dust storm began, indicating that it was about to rain. Having not consulted a map beforehand I didn't really have any idea where I was or how far from my destination I was.

As the dust began to dance more energetically, the boda-taxi driver pulled in under the roof of a petrol station for shelter. Other boda-taxi drivers were doing the same. By the time the rain began there were about forty or fifty men sheltering there – mostly boda-taxi drivers along with a few passengers, quite closely packed together in a small space. The body odour was almost overwhelming; I was not used to being in very crowded places during my time there.

What's more, if I wasn't uncomfortable enough with the smell, everyone was looking right at me. It was bizarre: I was near the middle of the crowd, with people pressing in on all sides, and everyone staring at me. They had no shame in it either – when I looked back nobody averted their eyes or pretended not to be staring; they just maintained eye contact.

I didn't speak to them – I was not confident in my Kinyarwanda and did not know whether any of them spoke any English. Nobody spoke at all, and I felt very awkward. I didn't know where to look, and ended up staring at the ceiling and staring out at the rain; trying to forget that forty or fifty pairs of eyes were watching me.

This came as a particular surprise to me because when I had been working in the office in Kigali, people's reaction to rain had been quite different. Whenever the 'dust began to dance', indicating that the rain was soon to come, everyone in the office would drop what they were doing and walk over to the windows. They would stand there in silence, looking out and watching the rain until it ended – at which point they would return to their work and their conversations.

I found it a wonderful tradition, though never discovered the reason behind it. So here, under this petrol station roof with so many boda-taxi drivers crammed in on all sides and looking straight at me, bizarrely enough *I* was the one staring at the rain. It was quite a relief when the rain stopped about half an hour later and we could resume our journey.

Part 6: Turkey

Stronger Ties

Hugged by soft light, another tea
Call to prayer rings through me again
Drenched in the blessing of sunset
And knowing the soft liberty of calm
Conscious of the brooding stillness.

Yet here crouches a hidden fear
Of the vehement, who paid in blood
And painted streets.

Removed from that pervasive stench
By culture, coincidence, confusion
Hoping to serve by using technology.
Distance that far exceeds language
Makes for very strange friendship

And yet stranger, stronger ties
Through blood that runs deeper still
As Family.

Chapter 6 – Turkey

The Journey to Istanbul

The journey from Rwanda to Turkey felt like a real test of endurance. There was a direct flight available from Kigali to Istanbul, but it would have cost £2,000 and I did not consider it worth the extra money – it was much cheaper to go the long way around. The cheapest way that I had found was to take a 12 hour daytime coach back to Kampala (Uganda); sleep there for a few hours and then fly to Nairobi (Kenya) the following morning; have eight hours in Nairobi and then fly to Brussels; fly from Brussels to London a few hours later (I don't remember which of the London airports it was); then fly on to Istanbul from there. It would take approximately three days in total.

So I set off from Kigali coach station, and the journey to Kampala was not dissimilar to the journey from Bujumbura to Kigali. The driver again appeared intoxicated, laughing loudly, singing and shouting a lot; speeding and swerving very close to the edges of the road, closely missing other vehicles as we passed. Perhaps this is normal for such coaches, but I found it nerve-racking and very uncomfortable.

When we crossed the border from Rwanda into Uganda I discovered that I needed a multiple entry visa in order to return to the country, which I had not considered. I was the only non-African person on the coach, and seemed to be the only one who did not speak much Kinyarwanda or Luganda –

so when we all had to alight at the border I did not quite understand what was happening. Everyone had to get off the coach and take passports and documents to a small outdoor booth.

I followed the crowd and queued at the booth, but was told that since I did not have a multiple-entry visa I would need to pay a sort of entrance fee to pass through. Unfortunately I didn't have enough Ugandan money left. I had some Ugandan shillings, some Rwandan francs and some Burundian francs – but not quite enough of either Rwandan or Ugandan money to be able to pay the total sum in one currency, and the border guards would not take the fee in a mixture of currencies or card payment.

Thankfully, a friendly man on the coach said that he would pay my entrance fee, and said I could withdraw more money at an ATM to pay him back when we arrive in Kampala. I felt slightly concerned about the idea of being indebted to this man until our night-time arrival, at which point he would follow me to an ATM in the middle of an unknown place. However, it seemed I had no other option.

When we finally got to Kampala I wandered around for over an hour looking for an ATM, with the stranger in silent pursuit. We finally found one. It happened to be in a rather dark and solitary place that made me a little nervous, but at least I was able to pay him back. I was very tired, frustrated, desperate for a shower, and did not particularly want to be in such a place at night with a bank card on show. But I repaid him, and then headed back to a well-lit main road unaccompanied.

By now I had about eight hours left in which to get to the airport. It was a little after midnight: the coach trip had overrun, despite the driver's speeding. Perhaps we had taken a detour. I hadn't arranged to meet anyone there as my plan was to go straight to the airport from the coach station and snooze on a chair there until the flight, assuming that public transport would be available from the coach station.

However, when I got to the coach station there were no boda-bodas or buses around. I ended up sleeping on the steps there until sunrise, hugging my rucksack. At first I was a little worried about safety, sleeping out in the open in a public space where there were no people around, but I was shattered and my body was aching all over from the coach trip. I fell asleep almost as soon as my head touched my rolled-up coat.

After sleeping for about four hours, I awoke to the sound of early-morning boda-bodas driving past and whistling at me. Before long the sun began to rise and the small buses started going past too. These are shaped like the little white vans that are common in the UK, but with benches in the back and can contain as many people as can physically squeeze their bodies into the space. Knowing that these are even cheaper to ride than the boda-bodas, I waved at one and asked the driver if he would be going to the airport. He said yes.

There were still about four hours before my flight was due to leave, and I knew it wasn't too far to the airport. Over the next hour and a half the driver didn't appear to be doing a set route – he simply seemed to go where the passengers requested, a little like a communal taxi. After my third time of asking whether we were anywhere near the airport, he said 'OK, OK, I will go there now.' Had he forgotten, I wonder, or was I simply a lower priority than those who had joined the vehicle after me? I didn't particularly mind; I wasn't in any hurry.

For some reason the driver didn't quite go to the airport. He took me as far as the end of a large road leading to it and then left, instructing me to 'go that way'. So I walked for half an hour or so, passing some solitary camels grazing at the side of the road. I wondered whether I had passed the airport without realising – or how much further I had to go.

Eventually a boda-boda drew up alongside me and offered to take me the rest of the way, for quite a high price. I bartered a little and a price was agreed. I was still reluctant to pay what felt like a lot for travelling down one road, but I didn't know how long it might take to walk the rest of the way and I now needed to be there fairly soon. On the boda-boda I realised that there were still several miles to go: I was relieved to have been able to catch a ride even though it used up all of my remaining Ugandan shillings!

When I got to the entrance a uniformed official approached me, as if I had been expected.

"Where are you flying?"

"Nairobi."

"Come with me. I will carry your bag."

"Please, I'd rather carry it myself. And I think I can make my own way to the gate, but thank you for offering."

"No – you must come with me. I will take you there safely." He took my bag from me by force, but I told myself not to make a fuss.

"Ok... Thanks. I don't have money to give you; I spent it all on the ride here."

"I don't want your money. Have you booked a checked bag, or will you be taking this into the place with you?"

"No checked luggage – I'll have my rucksack with me. Do I not need a boarding pass?"

"They will print it for you at the gate."

We walked along in silence for a while, until we reached the gate. There was a lengthy queue, and I started towards it.

"No, you come with me."

He led me to the desk at the front of the queue, said something to the member of staff at the desk who was about to begin checking people's documents, and put my rucksack down by my feet.

"Have a pleasant flight, Miss. He will see your passport

now."

"But why did I not have to queue like everyone else?"

The official laughed. "Mzungu!"

I stared at him open-mouthed as he walked away, shocked and horrified at once again receiving special treatment because of being white. Although I was the only 'Mzungu' on the flight I had assumed that at least in the airport I would be treated simply as human, like everyone else. I turned to the flight attendant, somewhat bewildered, hoping that he might explain this to me.

"I'm sorry – what's going on?"

He laughed. "Can I see your passport, Miss?"

"Erm, I think I'll go and wait at the back of the queue, actually. I'd be much happier queueing like everyone else." I picked up my bag.

"No, Miss. Your passport, please."

"But, why?"

"You are different to the others. Please, your passport."

I reluctantly handed it to him. He printed a boarding pass and waved me through with a bright smile, the first to board the flight. I felt so angry and couldn't understand how they could justify this. Why me? Had I missed something? Surely this kind of preferential treatment based on skin-colour couldn't be the policy – was it even legal? I pondered it throughout the flight, quite at a loss as to what could be done about it.

By the time I arrived in Nairobi I was very hungry. The last time I had had a meal was back in Rwanda. I had brought some snacks and water with me from there, and had finished them at the outdoor coach station in Uganda, which was now several hours ago. I wandered around until I finally found an ATM, once again in a somewhat dark and secluded area, just outside the Nairobi airport. I then realised that I had no idea what the exchange rate was, and could see no clues anywhere around me – nor any smartphone or computer access – so I simply withdrew the second-lowest amount that the ATM offered. *Please, God, make this enough for a meal and some water.*

The airport was beautiful, and I enjoyed walking around and admiring the lovely plants and artwork. The last gleam of orange in the sky faded into darkness and the chorus of the insects grew louder – it somehow felt like a very peaceful place. I was thankful for the time I'd been able to spend in this part of the world.

A group of taxi drivers shattered my sense of peace by shouting to me in English as I passed them, and whistling – one of them even offered to show me all around Nairobi on a four-hour tour for an amount of money that I didn't understand. It was a tempting offer. I had seven or eight hours to kill before my next flight, and was eager to see a little of the city. However, I could hear my Mum's voice in my head reasoning that it was probably unwise to get into a stranger's car at night, alone and with no awareness whatsoever of the country or culture or language. Anyway, my stomach was calling.

After buying a very refreshing meal at a little outdoor restaurant within the airport, with no idea how much I had spent but hoping it hadn't been too expensive, I went to the public loos and spent some time trying to wash as best I could from the sink. It was a struggle as I was trying to remain modestly clothed, due to the fact that the sink area was clearly visible from the doorway that led out into a public space. I wished desperately that there were a shower somewhere. Eventually I went to the gate, ready to board my flight to Brussels – the next stop on the way to Istanbul.

The flight was delayed. No amount of time was specified, and it ended up being more than three hours. As a result, by the time I got to Brussels I was only just too late to board my flight to London. And, frustratingly, I discovered that in order to be able to claim on travel insurance for missed flights I needed to have allowed over six hours for changeover time, which I had not done.

Disappointed and a little stressed, I realised that unless I could get an immediate flight to London I would also miss my flight from there to Istanbul. So, unable to find an affordable immediate flight to the right airport, I found myself wandering around Brussels airport asking at the different airline desks for their best offers regarding last-minute flights to Istanbul.

While I was doing so, I bumped into a man I recognised. He had recently moved to Burundi from the USA, and was volunteering at one of the projects that I'd visited.

"Oh, hi there Kathryn!"

"Hi! What are you doing here?"

He laughed. "Yeah, I remember telling you a few days ago that I'd be staying in Burundi for a couple of years. Well, my plans have changed – I'm heading into Europe for a while."

"Wow, that's sudden. What happened?"

"Let's just say a new adventure is calling to me."

"What about the project you were helping at?"

"They can cope without me. I'm never going back to Burundi. My home is the USA, not Africa. But I need a decent holiday before heading home."

I wondered what could have happened to spark this sudden change of heart. It gave me hope, though, that last-minute flights were indeed possible (I knew very little about air travel), and that I might therefore be able to get to Istanbul on time.

Finally, I found an airline that had a spare seat available on a flight to Istanbul. It was due to leave within the hour, and cost less me than a hundred Euros! I was delighted. I managed to contact my hosts in Turkey, letting them know that I would be arriving at around the same time as we had originally arranged, but at the other airport, on the European side of Istanbul rather than the Asian side. Having done little research, I seriously hoped that the airports were not too great a distance from each other.

After making this call I went straight to the gate. To my surprise it was empty: the other passengers had already boarded. Thankfully there was still someone at the desk, and I hurried over. Panting slightly, I handed her my passport and boarding pass.

"Hope I'm not holding people up or causing a delay!"

"No, don't worry." She looked at the passport and back up at me. Then she ripped up my boarding pass, printed off a new one and handed it to me along with my passport. "Here you are – have a nice flight."

"I'm not sure this is right – this boarding pass says Business Class. It's a different seat number to the one I bought at the desk – I didn't pay for a Business Class ticket."

"You have a free upgrade."

"Wow," I stammered. "I've never travelled Business Class before. Thanks!"

"No problem. Have a nice flight."

I boarded the plane, thankful, tired and excited. I also felt extremely out of place, surrounded by people in smart suits with laptops and iPads. It made me chuckle to wonder what the formal-looking businesspeople thought of me, a scrawny teenager in dusty African flip flops, skirt and t-shirt, sweating under an old green rucksack, with very greasy hair and huge bags under her eyes. As I settled in my large, comfortable seat, I was given a glass of Chardonnay and a stylish menu – it felt so surreal after the horrible coach journeys of recent weeks. I rather enjoyed that last leg of the journey to Turkey.

Never before or since have I appreciated a shower more than when I finally arrived at the house of my host family and was shown to their beautiful, clean bathroom. Such luxury. That night I slept better than I think I had ever slept before – the bed felt like the most comfortable one in the world, and I dropped off almost immediately.

First half

The plan was to volunteer at a church that had connections with the brother of a lady I met in the UK. I was staying and working in a suburb of Istanbul, on the Asian side. Since I didn't speak much Turkish I was limited in the ways that I could get involved – but I did help with a toddler group; led the music on guitar (singing in Turkish!) in a few house-based cell group meetings; did a lot of childminding so that parents could attend meetings and services; and helped with administration.

"You've come at an interesting time," my host told me one evening.

"Mm?"

"Next week is the annual sacrifice festival."

"What happens then?"

"It's a time of celebration for a lot of people. Families come together to worship Allah, and sacrifice animals to purge themselves and their families of evil."

"Really – people actually kill animals to cleanse themselves? I didn't realise that still happened nowadays."

"Yes, it happens. I'll tell you more about the animals and the process another day. For now, what you need to know is the family element. The streets may look deserted during the festival, but that's because everyone is indoors with their relatives. On the first day, people gather with their parents and siblings; on the second day with grandparents and cousins; on the third day with more extended family; then on the fourth day with friends or with any other relatives that they may have missed. It's a really important family time, and a time for relatives to encourage each other in their faith, too."

"Sounds great!"

"Well, yes – except for those who are no longer

welcome among their relatives for one reason or other: for those people it is an incredibly isolating and lonely week, full of shame and quite painful."

"Ah, I hadn't thought of that."

"For many of the people in our church, the festival is a really difficult time. Many of them have converted to Christianity from Islam, and as a result several of them have been cut off from their families. They are considered to be deserters – even betrayers – and to have brought great shame on their families by abandoning the faith they grew up in. So, some of them have not had any contact with relatives at all since leaving Islam."

"Wow, that must be really horrible."

"It is. And for a few people in the church, this festival is not only a shameful and isolated time but also a scary one. There are some whose particularly zealous relatives feel some kind of obligation to find the 'betrayers' and harm them in some way during the days of the festival. The threat is very real – for some this is such a terrifying week that they have to go into hiding until it's over."

"But if the relatives want to harm them, won't they just find a way to do so after the festival has finished, when they're out of hiding and back home?"

"Surprisingly, it seems not. The days of the festival are the crucial time – often people's houses or cars are targeted if the people themselves can't be found, so this is always a worry. But from our perspective the priority is keeping people safe, especially those that have received threats or have been attacked in previous years by family members or former friends."

"What can we do, then?"

"There are houses where people who fear for their safety can live during that week; usually together. So a major part of your work will be mundane things like getting groceries so that people don't need to leave the house if they feel unsafe doing so. But we'd also like to try to recreate something of the family celebration atmosphere. Many of these people consider the church to be their family now, and it would be good to find ways for people in the church to come together with food, stories, music, games and some cheerful activities together – making the most of the festival and sort of participating, in a different kind of way."

It was a very dramatic time, and not the sort of situation I'd ever really imagined. I found it distressing to think about the danger that people were in during that time, and heartbreaking knowing that some of these people had had no contact whatsoever with their families since leaving Islam. What a huge daily burden it must be. It was also very moving seeing all that people had given up for the sake of their Christian faith, and how much it must mean to them. Their devotion to it inspired and challenged me in my own faith.

I knew little about Islam, and asked many questions

throughout my time in Turkey – but didn't always understand the answers. So I tried to observe what was going on around me as best I could, without coming to too many conclusions about things that I didn't understand.

During the festival the church did try to recreate something of the family atmosphere and sense of celebration – a part of my role involved helping to transport church members to each other's houses and to or from the 'safe houses'. The beautiful music, incredible food, endless tea and long conversations were wonderful. However, it was not easy to forget the threats and fear still present in the backs of people's minds.

Second half

During the second half of the trip I was staying with a different couple, because the family I stayed with during the first week had unexpected family visitors. My new hosts were English teachers in a local language college, and had lived in Rwanda for several years before moving to Turkey. They had decorated their spare room with many beautiful Rwandan decorations. Several times I woke up confused as to which country and continent I was in – this happened many times throughout the year but was intensified when I was staying in that room. I kept somehow getting Kinyarwanda words into my broken Turkish sentences by accident, especially in the mornings.

I thoroughly enjoyed spending time with this couple.

They were full of fascinating stories of strange experiences and lessons learnt in many different parts of the world where they had lived – I loved to listen to them. One bizarre coincidence was that they had attended the college that by this point I had made up my mind to apply to. They happened to have an application form for my chosen course stored in the room where I was staying! I was baffled. They spent a considerable amount of time telling me how wonderful the lecturers were and what a fantastic place it is to study.

During this second half of my stay I was doing more or less the same sort of work as the first half: childcare, music, administration, errands and the like. Since the festival was over I was also able to spend some time in the homes of some of the people we had supported in hiding the previous week. I experienced such generous hospitality there.

I spent a lot of time on trains between my accommodation, the church, and people's houses. The trains were pleasant and I enjoyed the journeys. One particularly sticks in my memory: I heard someone speaking English, so I went over to say hello. I also thought that I vaguely recognised her, but couldn't think where from. It turned out that she was a musician and used to sing in a girl band that I listened to when I was about twelve – I had had posters of them on my bedroom walls! It would never have occurred to me that I might meet one of them on a train in Turkey.

On my day off each week I had chance to see some of the sights of Istanbul as recommended by my hosts and by

Turkish people I'd met. I got hopelessly lost in the spice market for quite some time – a fascinating and wonderful place! It was helpful that I understood a little Turkish by this point, so could ask for directions to different parts of the city without too much trouble. There were also various people that wanted to talk to me in English. One of these was with a lady selling things at a small stand on a street corner.

"What else are you doing while you are here in our country?"

"I'm helping out at a church, with various activities and groups as well as the services on Sundays."

"A church? What is it like?"

"Full of lovely people, of all ages. The services are quite lively, but I don't really speak enough Turkish to understand them very well."

She paused, frowning at me. "Why are the services in Turkish, not in English?"

"Erm, because almost all of the people that go there are Turkish."

"That can't be true. Turkish people are Muslim!"

Hmm, I thought. *And English people are Christians...?*

Part 7: Estonia

Tallinn

Shock of cold
Brutal and unforgiving in a land
Of tender company.

Depth of chat
Moments yet significant in a time
Of profound dialogue.

Sung tales shared
Abstract this community in a group
Of teenage creatives.

Thought-packed trip
Ponders still this extrovert in a mist
Of Tallinn's adventure.

Chapter 7 – Estonia

My time in Estonia was the only point in the year in which I was glad to have packed two jumpers. I had resented them so far: they added weight to my bag and reduced the amount of space in which I could squeeze chocolate or souvenirs. In all the other countries I was hot and sweaty, living in thin t-shirts. Anyway, now I needed the jumpers – badly. The average temperature in Tallinn in November is 1°, which was not at all what my body was expecting.

It was not my first time in the country – I had visited in the Christmas holidays of the previous year, and was glad to be back. The culture intrigued me, and hearing a little of Estonia's history in the first visit made me long to visit again and learn more.

The first trip had come about through a guest at the retreat centre where I worked in the Yorkshire Dales, who lived in Tallinn and encouraged me to visit. After some thought I accepted the invitation and brought two friends with me. We stayed for a week, volunteering for a small organisation that works to bring unity between people from different backgrounds across the city.

It was a fantastic week – we thoroughly enjoyed the hospitality, food and personalities of the people we met. We also saw in the New Year at the end of Tallinn's time as European City of Culture, and were present at the midnight firework display on Freedom Square, which was, and is still, the most impressive firework display I have ever seen.

Host Family

So I was eager to return, having been invited to come back and not 'work'. I was fortunate enough to stay with a family who had made a lasting impression on me on my first visit by being immensely loving and welcoming.

The woman of the house had extended a hand of friendship right from the first day of the previous visit and had kept in touch throughout the year in between. She was gentle and loving, and would often go out of her way to help people around her in various ways. What surprised me when I stayed with her was how eagerly she would watch me.

"Why do you look at me like that?"

"I hope to learn from you. I'm sure I can learn all kinds of things by watching how you live, how you talk and behave and do things each day."

I was quite bewildered. "Really? What could I possibly be, or have, or know, that anyone could learn by looking at me?"

She laughed. "Your life, like every life, is a wealth of knowledge and it is treasure to me. I want to take the opportunity to learn all I can."

Each day she would ask me about things that I did or said, little things that would in any other context go unnoticed. This certainly made me more self-aware – it challenged me to think before I speak, and to question why I do things the way I do. As well as learning more about myself, it made me want to start consciously watching, questioning and learning from other people too. However, I didn't necessarily want to do so as visibly as she did!

Through this time of being questioned and challenged to think quite deeply, and sometimes asking similar questions in response, I found it refreshingly easy to lay aside the shallow smalltalk that we Brits so comfortably fall back on. I never liked smalltalk anyway. The value of seeking to learn from those around us was imprinted on my mind through spending time with this wonderful woman.

As such, by the end of my stay I had started to see more or less every conversation as significant in some way – something to learn from or be challenged by; something to remember. I began seeing conversation as a tool not just for basic social interaction but also at times for deeper connection, real learning – like a spade digging into the ground of reality.

The knowledge that each person's mind and life is a whole world – stories, lessons learnt, experiences – excited me tremendously. It felt like a massive paradigm shift; a new way of engaging with life. Even one-off conversations with strangers and semi-strangers may have the potential to be lifechanging. It also helped that the vast majority of people in

Tallinn younger than 40 spoke at least a little English, as my Estonian wasn't up to much!

Living Room

A considerable amount of my time in Tallinn was spent in a fantastic new café a short walk from Freedom Square, called the Living Room. It was very trendy, full of arty decorations and musical instruments, and run by people in their 20s. There was a relaxed and informal atmosphere – often the staff would even give a meal or drink to a customer for free just because they felt like it.

It seemed to be the sort of place where anyone could talk to anyone, too: there was a sort of social freedom there that seemed quite unusual. There was a sense of community and acceptance; the sort of space that in some strange way you feel very much a part of even if you only visit a few times. I felt quite at home!

Here, I had lots of opportunity to practice my newfound love of conversations that reach some depth and touch on what life really means to people, by asking simple questions and expecting honest answers. It seemed I wasn't alone in this pursuit, this exploration, either. I had the privilege of meeting various people from different backgrounds and hearing about parts of their lives – it was wonderful to be able to make time to do so.

The couple that owned the café were fascinating people, too. It had only been open a few months at the time of my visit, and the couple had moved to Tallinn from a city in Russia where they had opened a similar student music café that had now been passed on to local people. Their enthusiasm for the student arts-and-music scene, and the part that the café could play in it, was hugely inspiring.

Through the café I also met various creative teenagers, who invited me to spend some time with them in their various hang-out places. One was a singer-songwriter who often did concerts and events; another an artist who did lots of strange but beautiful abstract pictures; another a sketcher who worked with pen and ink and produced some impressive pieces. They were relaxed and friendly, easy to talk to and eager to make new friends too.

This group of girls, along with a few other friends, spent much of their time organising things – bringing people together around art and music; even teaching people of different ages various creative skills and hobbies. It was refreshing to meet teenagers who were taking some sort of ownership of the community rather than expecting the grown-ups to put things on for them all the time.

Together with others in the city they had started small art groups, music groups and local events that seemed to be taking off. Their stories were inspiring, and I enjoyed hearing about things they had done and what they had learnt in the process. From what I heard, they also seemed to be inspiring and encouraging other people their age to think and act in a similar way, imagining what might be possible and refusing to be held back by their age or what people might think of them.

*****

Finally, after emotional goodbyes to various Estonian friends at the airport, I returned to the UK for a week or so to rest and collect my visa for Bolivia. During this time I didn't have chance (or money!) to venture up North to see my family: it was easier to stay in the Midlands with Ben's parents (who later became my in-laws), and I had a good time getting to know them better.

I was glad to have a few days to think back over the past six or seven months and process some of my experiences before launching into the next adventure. I was now very excited about the Bolivia trip, having waited and planned for it for six years. Alas – the stories and memories I have from Bolivia will have to wait for another time!

FAQ

I must take the opportunity to answer some of the questions that I am asked most frequently…

Where did the idea for this 'gap year' come from?

It all started when I was twelve years old and realised that I wanted to live abroad long-term. I remember my Mum telling me one day while she was preparing dinner that no cross-cultural organisation would employ me if I had no cross-cultural life experience – so, at twelve, I decided that I would take a gap year when I finished secondary school, to gain whatever experience was necessary.

I was in touch with a charity that worked with street children in various parts of Latin America, and Bolivia had stood out to me. So, I wrote to them and asked if I could volunteer for their project for a year when I turn eighteen, in about six years' time. They put me in touch with another organisation that would be able to equip and send me to Bolivia for the year. This became the plan – a year in Bolivia working with street children – which I then worked towards and dreamed of throughout my teenage years. Of course, what ended up happening was quite different!

How could I afford it?

The charity that were due to send me to Bolivia told me that it would cost £7,000 plus flights and insurance. I took on part-time work that I could do flexibly in the evenings, weekends and holidays, and doing odd jobs to collect money together.

Later, when the organisation told me that the total amount actually came to £13,000 – not £7,000 – I began planning and organising fundraising events of various kinds. I enjoyed all this, learnt many life skills and got a variety of useful work experience. Finally, after six years, I just about had the full amount, through working part-time jobs, being incredibly stingy and holding fundraising events with the help of some fantastic friends.

What happened – why did I not go to Bolivia for the full year?

Not long before I was due to fly to Bolivia, after five or six years of planning, learning Spanish, fundraising, working and researching Bolivian culture, I got a call from the organisation that was going to send me. They told me that since I had never before experienced Latin American culture, they were unable to send me there for the year after all; it was their policy. They said that since I had been so determined they hadn't realized that I had never been before.

Their proposed solution was to send me to Guatemala for a month with a small team in the Summer. Following this, I was to return to the UK for five or six months to process the experience, 'recover' from it and decide whether I still wanted to go for a longer time to Bolivia.

This conversation was incredibly stressful, having poured so much of my life into preparing to go to Bolivia. However, believing I had no choice in the matter, I agreed. I wondered how I would fill the five or six months in between, desperate not to have to get a full-time job in the UK during that time. I felt thoroughly embarrassed, especially after people had helped me with fundraising events and had supported me financially to get to Bolivia – and I couldn't bear another five or six months of sitting around in England waiting to finally get there.

So I thought and prayed and stressed about what I might do to fill that time. I kept it to myself so as not to be inundated with 'helpful suggestions' from those around me, which I saw as a threat to my long-awaited independence. Within a short time I received various invitations to visit friends and contacts around the world.

How did I choose which countries to go to?

As a teenager one of my weekend/holiday jobs had been helping out with children's work (and some cleaning work) at a retreat centre, where I had opportunity to get to know people from a wide variety of cultures. One of the friends I made there was a girl from the Czech Republic, who invited me to stay in her country for a month to learn about the culture and volunteer somewhere. She said that all I would need to pay for is flights – that everything else would be covered. I knew very little about the Czech Republic and wanted to see her again, so I agreed to go.

Through Facebook I had been in touch with a Ugandan charity for a few years, following their posts and looking at photos and stories on their page. I'm not quite sure how I first came across it. They ran orphanages, schools, health centres, educational events, development projects and the like. I was in touch with the leaders of the organisation and would talk with them every so often about things they were doing, quite inspired by their stories. A number of times they had invited me to come out to Uganda and visit them to see their work firsthand. Eventually I agreed to consider it – especially since I was hoping to visit Rwanda and so would be in East Africa anyway.

When I was in secondary school I had a rather eccentric head-teacher who seemed to enjoy calling people out of lessons whenever he could come up with a reason. He knew I had an interest in other cultures, so when a former pupil came to visit who had moved to Rwanda to work for a charity, he called me to his office to meet her. We kept in touch, and later she invited me to come and stay with her in Rwanda to help out for a while. Knowing that I would have some free time and would love to see that part of the world, I agreed.

I had been interested in Burundi for some time, because I had come across an English man who had lived and worked there for several years. I had attended a number of his talks when he visited the UK, and had talked with him at the end of each of them (did I mention that I like to meet people?). For a few years I was in semi-regular contact with him, and met his wife and children a couple of times. One day he invited me to come and stay with them in Burundi to visit the projects that he worked for. Since I was planning a trip to East Africa anyway, I agreed.

I had read a few stories about Turkey and had heard many fascinating things about the culture. When someone I met told me that her brother lived in Turkey and worked for a church there, I became very interested both in the culture and in the differences between English and Turkish churches. I was put in touch with the brother and his family, and was later invited to come and visit them and volunteer there for a while – so I agreed.

I had volunteered for a local charity in Estonia for a week in my Christmas holidays six months before finishing Sixth Form, and I loved learning about their culture. One of the guests who had visited the retreat centre I mentioned had put me in touch with a charity there. When people invited me to return the following December I jumped at the opportunity.

The stories of my experiences in Bolivia, when I finally got there, aren't to be found here in this little book – perhaps they'll come out later on. Watch this space!

Post-script

I do hope you've enjoyed these memories, observations and musings about my initial experiences of a few different cultures. There is so much more to tell – so many stories of things that happened and individuals I met; mistakes I made and lessons learnt – but a taster is sufficient for now. The trips have hugely shaped my outlook on life and the ways in which I make decisions, and I would strongly recommend this sort of travel to anyone and everyone: not simply staying in tourist hotels and seeing the sights of different countries, but lodging with residents where possible and getting involved in the life and work of local organisations; getting to know a little of the traditions, the stories and challenges of real life. I wish I had more time to learn about each of these fascinating cultures – I barely scraped the surface of understanding each place. As I write this, years later, I am still hoping that Ben and I will one day live and work long-term somewhere totally different to what we know and love in the UK, wherever that may be – and will be able to explore the personality of the culture in much more depth. We'll see where life's journey will lead!

Do get in touch if you'd like to chat about your own stories, insights, memories or hopes relating to different cultures – I'd love to learn from you and hear about your experiences! Email k.solidfoundation@gmail.com.

An eclectic collection of poems – many of them about the Christian life and its joys and struggles; some about the seaside, and various others more miscellaneous. Deep, and silly, and all in between.

Available now on Amazon: kindle or paperback.

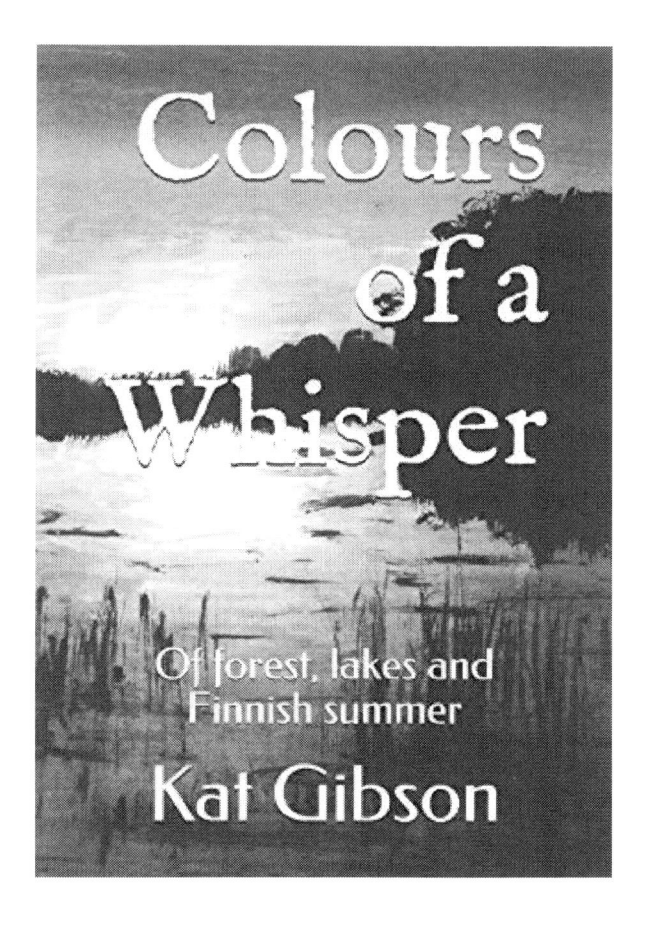

Not quite poetry in any strict sense, but these woodland musings might be regarded as almost poetic in style and tone. Whatever they are or aren't, may these ponderings bring a tiny piece of Finland into your life.

Available now on Amazon (paperback or Kindle).

Printed in Poland
by Amazon Fulfillment
Poland Sp. z o.o., Wrocław